W9-CAG-112

DISCARDED

RACHEL CARSON

LITERATURE AND LIFE SERIES
(Formerly Modern Literature and World Dramatists)
GENERAL EDITOR: Philip Winsor

Selected list of titles:

JOAN DIDION   *Katherine Usher Henderson*
LOREN EISELEY   *Leslie E. Gerber and Margaret McFadden*
T. S. ELIOT   *Burton Raffel*
ELLEN GLASGOW   *Marcelle Thiébaux*
C. S. LEWIS   *Margaret Patterson Hannay*
MARIANNE MOORE   *Elizabeth Phillips*
THE NOVELS OF HENRY JAMES   *Edward Wagenknecht*
CHRISTINA STEAD   *Joan Lidoff*
J. R. R. TOLKIEN   *Katharyn F. Crabbe*
LIONEL TRILLING   *Edward Joseph Shoben, Jr.*
GORE VIDAL   *Robert F. Kiernan*
SIMONE WEIL   *Dorothy Tuck McFarland*
EUDORA WELTY   *Elizabeth Evans*
OSCAR WILDE   *Robert Keith Miller*

*Complete list of titles in the series available from
publisher on request.*

90-91-168

5/17/90

23.32

921
Car

RACHEL CARSON

Carol B. Gartner

FREDERICK UNGAR PUBLISHING CO.
NEW YORK

Copyright © 1983 by Frederick Ungar Publishing Co., Inc.
Printed in the United States of America

Library of Congress Cataloging in Publication Data

Gartner, Carol B.
  Rachel Carson.

  (Literature and life series)
  Bibliography: p.
  Includes index.
  1. Carson, Rachel, 1907–1964. 2. Ecologists—United
States—Biography. I. Title. II. Series.
QH31.C33G37 1982   574′.092′4 [B]   82-40285
ISBN 0-8044-5425-6
ISBN 0-8044-6177-5 (pbk.)

Acknowledgments

I am grateful to Pace University in New York for supporting my research with a sabbatical leave and Kenan Grants.

During that research, Shirley A. Briggs, of the Rachel Carson Council, was particularly helpful in providing materials, contacts, and perspective.

The excerpt from Rachel Carson's letter to Dr. George Crile, Jr., is published by permission of Frances Collin, Literary Trustee.

To my three generations of fond supporters,
Mother and Dad
Larry
Alex and Madeline

Contents

Contents

Chronology

1907   Is born on 27 May in Springdale, Pennsylvania, to Maria McLean and Robert Warden Carson; sister Marian is ten, brother Robert, eight.

1918   Story "A Battle in the Clouds" is published in *St. Nicholas* magazine in the section for young authors; receives ten dollars.

1919   Has two more stories, "A Message to the Front," and "A Famous Sea Fight," published in *St. Nicholas*.

1925   Graduates from Parnassus High School, after attending Springdale Grammar School and two-year Springdale High School. Awarded scholarship to attend Pennsylvania College for Women in Pittsburgh (now Chatham College).

1929   Receives B.A. in science magna cum laude from Pennsylvania College for Women, where she has contributed to student newspaper, *The Arrow*, and literary supplement, *Englicode*. Awarded fellowship for summer study at Woods Hole Marine Biological Laboratory, and one-year scholarship for graduate study in zoology at The Johns Hopkins University. Sees ocean for first time.

1930   While continuing studies, works as laboratory assistant to Dr. Raymond Pearl, geneticist at Johns Hopkins. Family moves to house near Baltimore so she can live at home.

1930–36 Is teaching assistant in biology for Johns Hopkins summer sessions.

1931–33   Is half-time assistant in zoology at University of Maryland.

1932   Receives M.A. degree in zoology from Johns Hopkins.

1935   Father dies 6 July. To support her mother and herself, gets part-time work writing radio scripts for United States Bureau of Fisheries.

1936–39   After scoring first in civil service examination, gets permanent appointment as junior aquatic biologist at Bureau of Fisheries. With mother, moves to Silver Spring, Maryland. After death of elder sister Marian, they take in her two daughters. Occasional articles published in *Baltimore Sunday Sun*.

1937   "Undersea" published in *Atlantic Monthly*; considerable notice and acclaim.

1939–49   Articles in *Nature Magazine, Collier's, Coronet, Transatlantic, Field and Stream*, and other magazines.

1941   First book, *Under the Sea-Wind*, published.

1946   Is now aquatic biologist and assistant to chief of Office of Information of United States Fish and Wildlife Service (Bureau of Fisheries and Bureau of Biological Survey merged in 1940 to form Fish and Wildlife Service).

1942–43   Moves briefly to Chicago with Office of Information for wartime work.

1943–45   Writes and edits government booklets to promote eating of fish for purposes of wartime conservation of resources.

1947–50   Prepares "Conservation in Action" series for Fish and Wildlife Service; writes at least four herself.

1949   Appointed editor-in-chief for Fish and Wildlife Service. Experiences undersea diving; then deep-sea voyage to Georges Bank on government research ship. Receives Eugene F. Saxton Fellowship to complete work on *The Sea Around Us*.

1950   Wins George Westinghouse Science Writing Award for "The Birth of an Island," chapter of *The Sea Around Us* published in *Yale Review*.

1951   Awarded Guggenheim Fellowship for work on next book. Condensation of nine chapters of *The Sea Around Us* appears in June *New Yorker*; book published in July; voted "outstanding book of the year" in *New York Times* Christmas poll.

1952   Wins National Book Award for best nonfiction book of 1951 and John Burroughs Medal for natural history book of outstanding literary quality. *Under the Sea-Wind* is republished in April, joining *The Sea Around Us* on best-seller list. Receives honorary doctorates from Pennsylvania College for Women, Oberlin College, and Drexel Institute for Technology; made Fellow of the Royal Society of Literature in England. Resigns from government job.

1953   Receives honorary doctorate from Smith College and is elected to National Institute of Arts and Letters. Buys land in Maine; builds summer cottage overlooking water. RKO film *The Sea Around Us* wins Oscar as best full-length documentary of the year.

1955   Parts of *The Edge of the Sea* appear in *The New Yorker* prior to book publication. National Council of Women of the United States cites book as "outstanding book of the year"; wins Achievement Award of American Association of University Women.

1956   Writes script for "Omnibus" television program on clouds; "Help Your Child to Wonder" appears in *Woman's Home Companion*.

1957   When niece Marjorie dies, adopts her five-year-old son Roger Christie. Builds new home in Silver Spring.

1958   "Our Ever-Changing Shore" appears in *Holiday* magazine special issue, "Nature's America." After long illness, mother dies in December.

1960   Has tumor removed; is told she has cancer.

1962   After three-part condensation published in *The New Yorker*, *Silent Spring* appears. Chemical industry mounts personal as well as scientific attack. By end of year, there are over forty bills in state legislatures to regulate pesticides.

1963   Receives Schweitzer Medal of Animal Welfare Institute and Conservationist of the Year award from National Wildlife Federation. "CBS Reports" television show, "The Silent Spring of Rachel Carson," lets her air views along with representatives of chemical industry and government; President's Science Advisory Committee confirms facts and vindicates statements in *Silent Spring*. In December, receives medals from National Audubon Society and American Geographical Society; elected to American Academy of Arts and Letters. Writes foreword for Ruth Harrison's *Animal Machines*, book depicting cruelties of intensified methods of raising livestock.

1964   Dies 14 April in Silver Spring, Maryland, of cancer and heart disease.

1965   "Help Your Child to Wonder" reprinted as book, *The Sense of Wonder*.

1970   Rachel Carson National Wildlife Refuge in Maine dedicated by Secretary of the Interior Walter J. Hickel.

1980   President Jimmy Carter awards posthumous Presidential Medal of Freedom, the highest civilian award of the government, to Rachel Carson.

1981   Rachel Carson stamp issued by the United States Post Office, 28 May, in Springdale, Pennsylvania.

1

Scientist as Artist

If you mention the name Rachel Carson in conversation, those who know of her will answer, *"Silent Spring."* Pushed for a second response, they might supply "pesticides," for Carson's quietly explosive book started a worldwide environmental revolution. *Silent Spring* (1962) provided the first clear public statement of what pesticides, used without proper knowledge or controls, were doing to our environment.

Yet Rachel Carson was neither a protester nor what we have since come to call an environmentalist. For most of her professional life, she was a marine biologist who wrote so successfully about the sea that each of her three fact-filled yet beautiful sea books was a long-term bestseller, although the first, *Under the Sea-Wind* (1941), attained this status only when reissued (1952) after the phenomenal success of *The Sea Around Us* (1951).

No one has denied that Carson's literary talent greatly contributed to her success. In fact, the strongest attackers of *Silent Spring* complained that her superb writing made her more dangerous. Nevertheless, she is placed in the field of science or natural history, rather than literature. Detractors remember her only as a good nature writer, or perhaps a skilled propagandist or effective popularizer of science.

When she accepted the John Burroughs Medal for *The Sea Around Us*, she expressed "a certain awe and even

a sense of unreality" at being associated with "the im-
mortals" in nature writing—to her, American writers
Henry Thoreau and John Burroughs, and British authors
Richard Jefferies and W. H. Hudson.[1] But even her earliest reviewers had noticed the rare skill with which she
blended science and art, while at least one award, the
Burroughs Medal, recognized the outstanding literary
quality of her books.

I believe it is time to reconsider Rachel Carson's
work and restate the nature of her accomplishments. It
was because of their literary qualities that vast numbers
of people eagerly read her books, learned from them not
only facts but attitudes, and came to accept her radical
premises. Rachel Carson was above all a literary artist
whose subject was science, a perfectionist both in the
clear communication of facts and ideas, and in the use
of sounds, rhythms, images, and form.

Carson herself believed that there is "no separate
literature of science." "The aim of science," she said, "is
to discover and illuminate truth. And that, I take it, is
the aim of literature. . . ."[2]

She had planned from childhood to be a writer, but
when she discovered a greater interest in science at college, both she and those around her thought she had
changed the direction of her life. "Eventually it dawned
on me," she commented later, "that by becoming a biologist I would be giving myself something to write
about."[3]

The abilities that brought excellence to her writing
stem from the same talents that nurtured in her the gifted
scientist: fertile imagination and a keen capacity for original insights; acuity of observation with an eye for detail,
balanced by a sense of broader significance; honesty,
courage, and the patience for meticulous work, whether
in the field, in the laboratory, in the library, or at the
typewriter. To these talents, she added the ability to
practice science and literature as a single art.

Carson belongs with the few nonfiction writers admitted to the classic curriculum of American letters: de Crèvecoeur, with *Letters from an American Farmer*, Emerson, with *Nature* and other essays, and Thoreau, with *Walden* and the journals, among them. Like writers she admired, such as Melville, Conrad, and the nature writer Henry Beston, Carson fused words and rhythms into masterful prose, creating a living presence we can still enter.

Unlike most nonfiction writers, particularly those who write on scientific subjects, she sought to reach her readers through feelings as well as intellect. Her unique ability let her do all this while imparting factual material of considerable sweep and detail.

Although each of Carson's books is a separate literary work, they form a developmental thematic sequence reflecting her growing sense of ecological relationships and increasing forboding at the effect of our destruction of the natural world.

One can, of course, read any of the books alone, or study them in any order. Most of Carson's readers came to *The Sea Around Us* before reading *Under the Sea-Wind*, while many knew her first through *Silent Spring*, finding the book no less devastating because of a lack of previous acquaintance. Nevertheless, one best appreciates her accomplishments after reading the four books in order, followed by *The Sense of Wonder* (1965), an excellent summary of her philosophy that was originally (1956) a magazine article.

Carson believed that content must determine structure, a concept known in poetry as "organic form." "The subject takes command," she wrote, "and the true act of creation begins."[4] For each of her books, she found a new approach. *Under the Sea-Wind* is narrative, presenting information through storytelling, *The Sea Around Us* is straight exposition, while *The Edge of the Sea* (1955) is closer to the personal essay. *Silent Spring* takes the form of a documentary, incorporating techniques such as fable, case history, and scientific presentation as they are appropriate. Each book requires from us a different method of study. Only then can we assess Rachel Carson's work as a whole.

2

Nature and Books

The dominant influence on Rachel Carson's life and values was her mother, Maria McLean Carson, a minister's daughter who taught school until she married George Warden Carson from Pittsburgh. Maria Carson's own mother was also named Rachel,[1] suggesting her strong sense of mother-daughter bonds. Mrs. Carson and her daughter were close companions until the mother's death, barely more than five years before Rachel Carson's own. When Rachel Carson was at college, classmates called Mrs. Carson "the commuter," because every other weekend she visited the college; on alternate weekends, her daughter would go home.[2]

Another close relationship was with Marjorie, one of two teenage nieces Mrs. Carson urged that they take into their home after the death of the girls' mother, Rachel Carson's older sister Marian. Years later, when Marjorie died, Carson adopted her five-year-old son Roger.

During Rachel Carson's childhood, the family lived at the edge of Springdale, Pennsylvania, on sixty-five acres of land, adding ten more acres later. They did not farm, but there were animals—a cow, chickens, rabbits, pigs—and an apple orchard. In these surroundings, Maria Carson taught her daughter to love and study birds, animals, and plants.

A talented pianist and singer, Mrs. Carson often

5

played the piano for family sings, or read aloud to them in the evenings. She fostered her daughter's love for books, cultivated her sense of artistry and love of music, and encouraged her ambition to write.

In 1955, Carson summarized the events of her early life: "As a child, I spent long days out of doors in fields and woods, happiest with wild birds and creatures as companions. I read a great deal."[3] Although beaches later supplanted fields, these combined interests continued throughout her life. A college classmate writes that Carson was happiest on field trips, "her bobbed hair ruffled in the wind, her blue eyes intent and observing."[4] This love of the outdoors and always fresh delight in natural things was still evident at the end of her life, when she wrote glowingly of her joy in watching the migration of a flock of wild geese.[5]

At college, Carson reports, "my childhood interest in natural history found a new and clearer focus in the biological sciences." When later "the old desire to write began to reassert itself,"[6] she began a career stemming from these intertwined influences of childhood.

Work and leisure activities were not separate for Rachel Carson. "Since I like nothing better than to be within sight and sound of the sea," she wrote in 1951, "I find it impossible to draw a line between my avocations and my work. Ornithology is one of my hobbies that also contributes to my writing, and I consider few pleasures equal to early morning 'birding' during the spring migration season."[7] She made special plans to see or hear birds she was unacquainted with, like the veery, whose call later became a favorite. An active participant in the Audubon Society, Carson served as a director of the local chapter.

A recent critic finds Carson's fondness for birds "quite hard to square with a passionate love of cats!"[8] Carson declared that her "very closest nonhuman friends have been cats,"[9] but had no difficulty with loving both birds and cats. Next to a picture of her with her black cat Moppet in *Life* magazine is the comment, "My cats don't go outside much but if they did I imagine they'd take an occasional bird. . . . I regret the loss of a bird but I don't resent it. . . it's entirely a cat's nature to prey on birds."[10]

Her tremendous respect for life reflects her mother's teaching. Mrs. Carson would put spiders and other insects out of the house, rather than kill them. When her mother died, Rachel Carson wrote to a friend, "Her love of life and of all living things was her outstanding quality, of which everyone speaks. More than anyone else I know, she embodied Albert Schweitzer's 'reverence for life.'"[11] Rachel Carson's brother remembers their mother's disapproval when he shot rabbits, although she never failed to dress and cook them.

In publications for the United States Fish and Wildlife Service, Carson accepts the policy that hunting is a valid use of government land, even of wildlife refuges, when kept in proper balance. But she personally detested blood sports. "When she detected in the writing of others what she considered a 'glorification of cruelty,'" biographer Paul Brooks writes, "she was moved to cold anger."[12] Writing about experiences on a government research ship, she describes the beauty of "slender shapes of sharks moving in to the kill." "When some of the men got out rifles and killed them for 'sport,'" she comments, "it really hurt me."[13]

Friends tell dramatic stories about how she always returned specimens to the places in the ocean where she had found them, often waiting for the proper moment in the tide, and picking her way late at night down to the shore. She returned specimens whenever possible, according to her colleague Shirley Briggs, but Briggs believes this reputation for benevolence has become as exaggerated as the attacks on her reliability after the publication of *Silent Spring*.[14]

Maria Carson also influenced the development of her daughter's independent value system, stressing that intellect and a sense of personal worth were more valuable than social success.[15] Financial success was important to Carson only for the possibilities it offered, such as a life devoted to writing and a cottage on the coast of Maine. Even when her reputation was at its highest, she consistently refused to endorse products.[16]

The family's living situation encouraged acquaintance with nature, but restricted Carson's opportunities for friendship. Biographer Philip Sterling reports that she "did not make friends readily or carelessly," and childhood companions felt they were "subject to Mrs. Carson's approval."[17] Throughout her life, Carson remained shy and reserved, apparently avoiding intimate relationships, although she always showed concern for others. A classmate remembers how Carson corrected the impression that their biology teacher purposely ignored students in the halls. "Rachel said, 'Speak to her when you see her, she is very near-sighted and doesn't even see you.' It was true."[18]

There is little evidence of male friends during Carson's college years. In letters from that period, she mentions only one big date, for her junior prom. References to men in letters written while she was in graduate school merely describe competition in laboratory work. Her comment to an interviewer that she never married "because I didn't have time" is often quoted, but there is no reason to believe that she ever wanted to marry, even though she wrote sympathetically to a college friend about the difficulties of marrying during the depression.[19]

Paul Brooks comments that Maria Carson urged Rachel to take on family responsibilities—her sister Marian's two young daughters, and later Marjorie's son—but, he concludes, "it is probably an understatement to say that Maria Carson never urged Rachel to marry."[20]

People who worked with her remember her "wonderful mind." Her memory was "so keen she could quote almost verbatim the paragraph she had dictated a few days earlier."[21]

Although Carson wrote poems from the age of eight, none was ever accepted for professional publication. At ten, her first story was accepted by *St. Nicholas* magazine, followed shortly by two others. She later declared that she "turned professional" at twelve or thirteen "by selling to *St. Nicholas* a little piece I had written about the magazine. The pay, I believe, was a cent a word."[22]

Few students at the Pennsylvania College for Women were interested in serious work, but the school was highly proper, acceptable to her mother, and offered Carson a small scholarship and private financial help. She entered as an English major, intending to become a writer. Even though she had never seen the ocean, her first story for the literary magazine had a seacoast setting.

Through an unusual teacher, Carson discovered the excitement of biology and found that the pull of science had become stronger than that of literature. College administrators and classmates wholeheartedly disapproved of her change in major, pointing out that there was no future for women in science, outside of teaching in high schools or out-of-the-way colleges. Only in writing could a woman hope for real success. Even Carson addressed a fellow science student as "Mr. Collector," when she wrote asking her to bring specimens of comb jellies and Portuguese men-of-war back from Florida. The desire to write never really disappeared. Carson jokes in another letter to the same friend about the book they were going to write on the genetics of Carson's tailless cats.[23]

A fellowship at the Woods Hole Marine Biological Laboratory the summer after graduation gave Carson a chance to travel and see the ocean, which had fascinated her since childhood. She found the demanding research a fine experience, writing that she could easily develop the habit of going there every summer. She showed her usual practicality, however, by adding that it would be more valuable for her to spend the following summer teaching somewhere.[24]

Before beginning her graduate work, Carson went to Washington to consult with Elmer Higgins, head of the Division of Scientific Inquiry at the United States Bureau of Fisheries. This began the pattern she later established of always identifying and consulting with experts. She questioned Higgins about research in marine biology, what she should study, and possibilities in the field for women.

Financial problems and difficulties with experimental animals delayed Carson's completion of her graduate work, but she finally finished her dissertation, "The Development of the Pronephros During the Embryonic and Early Larval Life of the Catfish (Inctalurus Punctatus)," receiving her master's degree from The Johns Hopkins University in June, 1932.

Even though Carson did not marry, family responsibilities always prevented a carefree life. "When she had the money and could have traveled," Shirley Briggs commented, "then she had the domestic ties that kept her from doing it."[25] When her father died in 1935, she became responsible for her own support and that of her mother. Mrs. Carson kept house, helped with correspondence, and did her daughter's typing, but Rachel Carson earned their living. Later, when her mother was old and ill, Carson took on the responsibility of caring for her.

Carson continued her teaching assistantships after graduation, but additional work was difficult to find during the depression years. She again visited Elmer Higgins at the Bureau of Fisheries. By chance, he had part-time work available for a scientist who could write, preparing radio scripts for the bureau.

After Carson scored first in the civil service examination for a permanent position, she was appointed, at Higgins's request, to his office. She rose steadily in government service, writing and editing publications ranging from the *Progressive Fish-Culturist*, a widely circulated professional journal, to booklets urging Americans to eat more fish.

As an editor, she never tolerated shoddy work or technical jargon. Shirley Briggs, who worked with her at the Bureau of Fisheries, summarizes her accomplishments there: "Ruthless with her own writing, she tried equally to raise the standards of the federal prose she dealt with. . . . The tact and skill with which she tackled uninspired writers was a joy to watch. Her private views were often more pungent."[26]

Carson's own government writing shows liveliness, care, and a sense of style unusual in such materials. Her greatest contribution was a series of booklets promoting government efforts to establish wildlife refuges, needed to curb growing losses of wild birds and prevent destruction of the few remaining unspoiled marshlands. Coining the title "Conservation in Action" for the series, she produced publications that are pleasing both to read and to look at, with attractive formats and paper, and bold, effective illustrations. They show how good government publications can be.

Carson herself wrote four of the booklets, including the first, a delightful description of "Chincoteague, A National Wildlife Refuge" (1947), off the coast of Virginia. The fifth booklet of the series, "Guarding Our Wildlife Resources" (1948), spells out the ecological philosophy implicit in the earlier pamphlets.

To bring in needed additional income, Carson began contributing feature stories to the Sunday magazine of the *Baltimore Sun* soon after beginning her government work. Stories covered shad fishing, marine topics like "Numbering the Fish of the Sea" and "Farming Under the Chesapeake," and conservation-oriented topics such as "Mecca for Conservationists" and "Terrapin Now Multiplying." She rarely received more than ten or fifteen dollars each. Passages from some of the articles, such as a story on eels, reappeared later in *Under the Sea-Wind*.

Beginning a few years later, she was able to add to her income by writing magazine articles and book reviews. Her subjects were mainly birds and ocean life, but one wartime piece printed in both *Collier's* and *Reader's Digest* clearly explains what radar is, declaring that "The Bat Knew it First."[27] The Navy liked the piece so much that they reprinted it for recruitment purposes.[28]

Her independent professional writing career had started when her chief, Elmer Higgins, asked her to prepare an introduction for a booklet based on her "fish-story" radio scripts. Carson wrote a piece so evocatively beautiful that Higgins told her it was unsuitable. After requesting a simpler introduction, he suggested she send the original piece to the *Atlantic* foremost of literary magazines. To her surprise, starting at the top worked. The *Atlantic* published "Undersea" in 1937.[29]

Their "Contributor's Column" pointed out the unusual sense of presence already evident in Carson's work: "Ever since Jules Verne's imagination went twenty thousand leagues deep, people have wondered what it would be like to walk on the ocean's floor. Rachel L. Carson . . . has a clear and accurate idea."[30]

Carson packed a remarkable amount of information into four lyrical pages. Her concepts of the ecological relationships among all living things and their environments, and the continuous recirculation of resources, dominate "Undersea" as they do her later work. She anticipates her sea books when she writes of sharks' teeth and the ear bones of whales found at the bottom of the deepest parts of the sea. These become her symbol for enduring matter, remnants of creatures whose other elements have long since entered into "different incarnations in a kind of material immortality."[31]

Suggesting other themes of her later work, she identifies man as "chief, perhaps, among the plunderers," and writes in closing, "Against this cosmic background the life span of a particular plant or animal appears, not as a drama complete in itself, but only as a brief interlude in a panorama of endless change."[32]

"Undersea" brought Carson many letters and enthusiastic responses. Elmer Higgins had already suggested she write a book. The pattern, he assured her, was right there in "Undersea" ready to be filled in. Two correspondents made the same proposal. One was the famous historian Hendrik Willem van Loon, and the other, Quincy Howe, editor-in-chief at van Loon's publishers.

Carson worked on *Under the Sea-Wind* primarily at night. Colleagues at the bureau knew she was writing something, but when the book came out they were pleasantly shocked at its quality and beauty. Appearing only a month before the Japanese attack on Pearl Harbor plunged the United States into World War II, the book received favorable reviews but sold few copies.

Praise from fellow scientists and naturalists pleased Carson the most. Oceanographer William Beebe wrote in the *Saturday Review* that her science could not be faulted,[33] and the Scientific Book Club chose *Under the Sea-Wind* as a selection. Beebe included two chapters in his collection, *The Book of Naturalists, An Anthology of the Best Natural History* (1944).[34] Beebe began with Aristotle and ended with Carson, one of only two women represented, and the only one writing independently. The other woman was a coauthor with her father.

Under the Sea-Wind appeared in German as *Unter Dem Meerwind* (1945). Carson's graphic prose also reached the blind in Braille and Talking Books editions.

During the war years, Carson was increasingly occupied with government work, moving temporarily to Chicago one fall and winter when information personnel were transferred there to free office space in Washington. After the war ended, she tried to find an editorial position outside the government to avoid the constraints she felt government work imposed on her writing, but in the midst of the postwar job shortage she was unsuccessful. Remaining with the Fish and Wildlife Service, she was promoted to a higher editorial position, which gave her greater responsibilities but less time for her own writing and decreased opportunities for travel.

Throughout the war, Carson had been struck by the extensive new knowledge of oceanography being developed for military purposes. When this flood of material was no longer classified for security reasons, she began to plan a second, more comprehensive book about the sea. This would be the book van Loon had really wanted her to write when he asked what went on under the sea's seemingly lifeless surface.

Preparing *The Sea Around Us* required monumental research and organization. She often wondered why she had undertaken such a project, but managed to continue writing, even fitting in two adventurous forays into the sea. William Beebe, well known for his undersea explorations, had insisted that she could not write the book without getting herself beneath the surface of the ocean. With his help, she arranged to try diving with a helmet and lead weights in Florida, during the summer of 1949.

She had also wanted to see firsthand what the ocean was like from a ship at sea. Having already taken short cruises on Fish and Wildlife Service vessels, she convinced her superiors that she could deal more effectively with information from the research ships if she boarded one for a deep-sea voyage. One woman on shipboard with an all-male crew was not acceptable to the service, so she drafted her agent, Marie Rodell, to join her on the *Albatross III* for a ten-day trip to Georges Bank, a famous fishing ground south of Nova Scotia.

When Carson won a Eugene F. Saxton Memorial

Fellowship, she was finally able to take some time off from work to concentrate on her writing. She completed *The Sea Around Us* in two years.

Thanks to Marie Rodell's persistence, Carson was able to establish her pattern of publishing chapters in magazines prior to book publication. This produced both income and publicity, and in one case, an award. The appearance of "The Birth of an Island" in the *Yale Review* won Carson the George Westinghouse Science Writing Award of the American Association for the Advancement of Science.

The New Yorker published an extensive condensation as a three-part "Profile of the Sea." This was unusual material for that magazine but drew enthusiastic responses that contributed immeasurably to the success of the book. *The Sea Around Us* stayed on the best-seller list for more than eighty weeks, was translated into thirty-two languages, and was turned into a Golden Book for children. Its success was so dramatic that the publishers put out a new edition of the neglected *Under the Sea-Wind*, which promptly joined *The Sea Around Us* on the best-seller list.

Despite her shyness and modesty, Carson knew the value of honors and awards and prompted her publishers to make sure her book reached the proper hands.[35] Among other awards, she won the John Burroughs Medal for an outstanding book of natural history, and the National Book Award for nonfiction. She was also elected to the British Royal Society of Literature and, in the United States, the National Institute of Arts and Letters.

Carson was delighted when RKO bought the motion-picture rights for *The Sea Around Us*, but the resulting film was an embarrassment. She and Marie Rodell succeeded in having the worst errors corrected, but the script bore little resemblance to her book and had none of its magic. Nonetheless, the film received an Oscar as the best full-length documentary of 1953.

The success of *The Sea Around Us* transformed Carson into a literary celebrity. Although she was still painfully shy, she had to accept at least some public appearances. Marie Rodell described her first public talk at a book and author luncheon with fifteen hundred guests. "Miss Carson was 'scared to death,' but she plunged into the talk." She had brought along a recording of undersea sounds to take up some of the time.[36] Both the recording and Carson were a great success.

Even in college she had disliked public speaking, but, as a classmate commented later, her performance was usually better than she thought it would be.[37]

Invasions of her personal life were more difficult for her to accept. Readers even followed her under beauty parlor dryers or into motel bedrooms. Not anticipating the public clamor, her publishers had included no picture on the book jacket. This led readers to imagine a figure of protean proportions far different from the more modest reality. Her friend Shirley Briggs painted a portrait of a prodigious Rachel Carson "as her readers imagined her," complete with octopus. The picture hung in the Carson home, where Mrs. Carson used it to scare off unwanted household help.[38]

With success, Carson's correspondence multiplied. Frank Graham points out that she inspired "affection as well as respect among her readers," and responded to it by replying "with courtesy and thoroughness" to all her letters.[39]

The keen sense of humor Carson's friends always mention rarely appears in her public writing, although it is evident in letters and informal pieces.[40] Shirley Briggs believes that if you want to be taken seriously as a scientist, you cannot write with humor or your work will be discounted. If you are a woman and want people to pay attention to the seriousness of your subject, you must be particularly careful. Carson wanted to be taken seriously.[41]

Some readers of *The Sea Around Us* refused to believe the writer could be a woman. "Among male readers," Carson explained, "there was a certain reluctance to acknowledge that a woman could have dealt with a scientific subject." One correspondent, "who apparently had never read the Bible enough to know that Rachel is a woman's name," wrote to the author, "'I assume from the author's knowledge that he must be a man.'"[42]

Such reactions multiplied later, after publication of *Silent Spring*, when detractors attempted to discredit her work by labeling her a "hysterical woman." *Life* magazine, at that time, explained that she was "unmarried but not a feminist," a gallant attempt, perhaps, to save her from yet another unpopular label. The article quoted her comment, "I'm not interested in things done by women or by men but in things done by people."[43]

Despite this disclaimer, Carson was always conscious of her position as a woman and proud of her "firsts." "I receive the Audubon Medal Dec. 3," she wrote to a friend in 1963. "This is the 10th (or maybe 11th) time it has been given in 16 years, and the first to a woman." She called her election to the prestigious American Academy of Arts and Letters "about the most deeply satisfying thing that has happened in the 'honors department.' As you may know, membership . . . is limited to 50 . . . at present there are only three women. . . . [T]here seem never to have been more than about a dozen women. I truly never expected this to happen."[44]

She also labored to prevent gender-based dismissal of her beliefs, telling the National Council of Women of the United States, during the furor over *Silent Spring*, "There is something more than mere feminine intuition behind my concern about the possibility that our free wheeling use of pesticides may endanger generations yet unborn."[45]

Even favorable commentators diminished her accomplishments with sexually based comments. In his highly adulatory introduction to the British combined edition of Carson's three sea books, editor Brian Vesey-Fitzgerald writes: "It has been given to few women, other than the mistresses of emperors and kings, so to influence governments. It has, I believe, been given to no other woman to do so through the medium of a book." He broadens his admiration appreciably in the next paragraph, saying, "It is difficult to introduce genius: and that is what I am asked to do."[46]

The success of *The Sea Around Us* finally allowed Carson to give that "genius" free reign. She resigned from her government position in 1952 to devote herself full-time to writing. Her income now so far surpassed all obligations—including complete support of her mother, who needed medical care, and help to other members of the family—that she no longer needed the Guggenheim Fellowship which had been awarded to her for work on her next book, and returned the money.[47]

Carson no longer had to look for outlets for her writing. RCA Victor asked her to write album notes for a Toscanini recording of Debussy's *La Mer*, using the material for at least three different albums. Her essay not only reflected the beauty of her writing, but her ability to translate her insights about the sea into descriptions and analysis of the music.

Carson "lived" the production of her next book, *The Edge of the Sea*, exploring the seashores she was describing, and writing much of the book from her own research and experience. Houghton Mifflin had asked her to write a guide to the seashore, but in Carson's hands, the book evolved into a study of ecological zones between the tide lines.

This time, both *The New Yorker* and the *Reader's Digest* published condensations. Warmly praised by her fellow scientists, *The Edge of the Sea* remained on the bestseller list for more than twenty weeks and brought her more honors: an Achievement Award from the American

Association of University Women and a citation for "the outstanding book of the year" from the National Council of Women of the United States.

After her work on *The Edge of the Sea*, Carson took the time to complete a few brief projects. There was a television script for the respected "Omnibus" series, based on Dr. Vincent Schaefer's excellent films on clouds. Carson had little interest in television, but appreciated the opportunity to present her ideas to a large audience, and especially the opportunity to do it without a personal appearance. She dramatically portrayed the atmosphere as our second ocean for the program, "Something about the Sky," which appeared on 11 March 1956.

That August, "Help Your Child to Wonder" appeared in the *Woman's Home Companion*.[48] Carson drew on her own experiences teaching both her grandnephew Roger, and earlier, his mother, Marjorie, about nature. She planned to expand the article into a book. Even though she was never able to return to the project, the article was reprinted in book form as *The Sense of Wonder*, after her death.

She also wrote an article for *Holiday* magazine's special issue, "Nature's America," published in July 1958. "Our Ever-Changing Shore"[49] describes America's coastline, regaling us with lively details from history, geology, and biology.

Carson had long been aware of the dangers of DDT. As early as 1944, she had read scientists' warnings that its use would destroy beneficial as well as harmful insects and upset natural balances. Her colleagues at the Fish and Wildlife Service, Clarence Cottam and Elmer Higgins, had written of possible long-term consequences. In the 1950s, there were reports of DDT's effects on the "food chain," and how it is concentrated and accumulated in fatty tissues.

By 1958, Carson had various ideas for her next book, but most seriously considered writing on the ecology of

man for the Harper *World Perspectives* series. She planned
to include the problem of man's attacks on his environment, but not to single out pesticides. A letter from her
friend Olga Owens Huckins, formerly with the Boston
Post, began to change her orientation.[50] The Huckinses
had a private bird sanctuary in Duxbury, Massachusetts,
which had been doused with DDT when the state
sprayed surrounding areas in an attempt to control mos-
quitoes. Mrs. Huckins wrote to the Boston *Herald* graphically describing the agonizing deaths of her birds, after
state assurances that the spray was harmless. She expressed her outrage at this invasion of private land.

Because massive additional spraying was being proposed, Olga Huckins sent a copy of her letter to Rachel
Carson, asking her to search in Washington for persons
who might help prevent further spraying. Carson inves-
tigated, only to find the pesticide situation far worse than
she had believed—all she valued was being threatened.

Finding no one else who could or would make the
facts public, she decided she herself would write an article. When she found that most magazines would not
even consider publishing such an article, she knew she
had to write a book. The work on that book gradually
came to possess her, so that *Silent Spring*, published in
1962, less than two years before her death, became
Rachel Carson's last and most arduous undertaking.

At first it was to be a brief book, quickly written,
with a chapter published first as an article in *The New
Yorker*. But as Carson continued her inquiries, her information and her concern grew.

When citizens on Long Island sued the government
to protest aerial spraying of DDT over heavily populated
suburban areas to control the gypsy moth, the trial provided Carson with material for her research and many
of her first contacts. As her work continued, she met and
corresponded with experts from around the world, far
outdistancing the number of references she had gathered

for *The Sea Around Us*. That, she had thought previously, was the limit of her research.

Knowing that the topic was explosive and that pressures against her from pesticide-related industries and institutions would be tremendous, Carson was anxious not to let out too much information until her work was complete. One lead led to another; each fact invited further research. Her expected date of completion was continually deferred.

Care of her mother, seriously ill until her death in December 1958, slowed Carson's pace early in the work. The dislocation caused by her mother's death was compounded by responsibility for her adopted child, grandnephew Roger Christie.

She gathered information, wrote, rewrote, and meticulously checked each fact and interpretation, sending portions of the manuscript to experts in each field to be checked for accuracy. She wrote to her editor, Paul Brooks, that she was sustained by her conviction that when finally finished, the book would be "built on an unshakable foundation."[51]

As she worked, promotion of pesticides by industry and the United States Department of Agriculture increased, and sales grew, but there were glimmers of concern. President Kennedy called for an end to conflicting interests within the government, singling out pesticides as an example, while Congressman John Lindsay of New York asked the Department of Agriculture whether new laws were needed to fight environmental pollution. The department assured him they were not.[52] The need for clear public information became more urgent.

In the midst of her work on *Silent Spring*, Carson had to pause to revise *The Sea Around Us* for a new edition. She could not incorporate all the new research, only indicate its extent. She wrote a preface describing the changes and developments in oceanography, concluding with a strong declaration of the dangers of pollution.

Even the sea, she warned her readers, was threatened, and with it, all life.

After more than four years, *Silent Spring* was finally ready for publication. Paul Brooks effectively summarizes the struggle he viewed from his editorial vantage point.

She had wrestled with a book that grew like a living organism, spreading in unforseen directions, nourished by the mountains of research material that she had amassed. To give shape and beauty to her unpromising subject matter, to keep it down to manageable size, to bring out the clear pattern underlying the complex details, above all to bolster every statement against inevitable attack—this was a feat to be achieved only by a scientist who was also an artist.[53]

Clarence Cottam, a respected scientist and former colleague who had provided considerable help during Carson's research, had warned that she would be condemned and ridiculed. "Facts," he said, "will not stand in the way of some confirmed pest control workers and those who are receiving substantial subsidies from pesticide manufacturers." He warned also that a book on this subject could not be a best-seller.[54] This last prophecy was wrong, but the resistance he foresaw was as virulent as expected.

Again a long condensation appeared in *The New Yorker*, beginning on 16 June 1962 and continuing for two more issues. Public response was overwhelmingly favorable, with floods of letters to Congress, government agencies, and newspapers, as well as to *The New Yorker* and to Carson herself. A report in the Book-of-the-Month Club bulletin announcing their selection of *Silent Spring* was written by United States Supreme Court Justice William O. Douglas.

Carson traveled to Scripps College in California to give the 1962 commencement address. Her strong and stirring speech, "Of Man and the Stream of Time," reaffirmed her belief that man must no longer approach nature as an arrogant conqueror. If we do not act with wisdom instead of irresponsibility, she warned the graduates, the price of conquest may well be the destruction of man himself."[55]

Even before *Silent Spring*'s publication, Velsicol Chemical Corporation, a large manufacturer of pesticides, tried to intimidate the publishers into withdrawing the book by threatening a law suit over "inaccuracies" in descriptions of their products. The rest of the industry and those in universities, foundations, and agencies supported by the industry, waited for the book to be published in September. Not to seem on the defensive, they acted indirectly through book reviews by friendly scientists, parodies, manuals to their employees on how to combat *Silent Spring*, and barrages of publicity materials and "public information," what Carson called a "stream of booklets designed to protect and repair the somewhat battered image of pesticides."[56]

Most reprehensible were the personal attacks on Rachel Carson, attempts to impugn her credentials as a scientist, and accusations of inaccuracy, fanaticism, emotionalism, and insufficient documentation. Charges were noisy and widespread but unproven. Many of the critics had never even read the book they misrepresented. The charge of insufficient documentation is explicitly refuted by the long and specific list of references that appears in *Silent Spring* itself.

At Carson's death, *Time* magazine continued its attack, but in the calmer rhetoric of an obituary. The discussion of *Silent Spring* is a good specimen of this sort of criticism.

Despite her scientific training, she rejected facts that weakened her case, while using almost any material, regardless of authenticity, that seemed to support her thesis. Her critics, who included many eminent scientists, objected that the book's exaggerations and emotional tone played on the vague fears of city dwellers, the bulk of the U.S. population, who have little contact with uncontrolled nature and do not know how unpleasantly hostile it generally is. Many passages mentioned cancer, whose cause is still mysterious. Who knows? suggested the book. Could one cause of the disease be pesticides?[57]

Time also echoed the common misrepresentation that *Silent Spring* calls for an end to all use of pesticides and all chemical controls, a position Carson specifically repudiates in the book.

Many outstanding scientists admired and defended *Silent Spring*, but the strongest rebuttal of Carson's critics came from the President's Science Advisory Committee, specifically convened by President Kennedy to investigate pesticides. Their report substantiated all of Rachel Carson's facts and interpretations, affirming as she did that much more needed to be known.

Despite the controversy over *Silent Spring* and Carson's awareness of the need to reiterate and defend its facts and statements, her health limited her ability to make public appearances. She gave what talks and interviews she could and testified effectively on pesticide issues at congressional hearings.

She agreed to appear on television as part of the "CBS Reports" analysis of the pesticide situation and of the validity of *Silent Spring*. "The Silent Spring of Rachel Carson" set her comments against those of Dr. Robert White-Stevens of the American Cyanamid Company, who had been traveling throughout the country defending pesticides. There were statements also from government officials, including Secretary of Agriculture Orville Freeman.

Carson's emphasis was on the lack of sufficient knowledge about the effects of pesticides especially over the long term, for coherent planning. Neither the pesticide industry nor the government could prove that they really knew what they were doing. Carson's dispassionate factual statements, supported by admissions wrung from government spokesmen, left viewers with a strong tilt toward Carson's position, despite White-Stevens's intemperate attacks and continued misrepresentations.

By the spring of 1963, *Silent Spring* was already well known in England, where it was recommended by Prince Philip and cited in parliamentary debates. Reports of its contents and the publication of translations spread its impact through much of the world. Carson's health made it impossible for her to accept invitations to lecture in Europe. Shirley Briggs, who was traveling there, sent her reports on the great respect European scientists had for her, and their descriptions of the wonders being effected by *Silent Spring*, especially after its vindication by the President's Science Advisory Committee.[58]

Researchers and others already working to combat the abuses of pesticides were grateful both for the support and for the surge in public interest. Many governments moved to enact stronger controls. Frank Graham, Jr.'s *Since Silent Spring* describes the book's powerful effects in the years up to 1970, but he concludes that the problem of pesticide contamination has worsened since Carson's death, despite the considerable impact of *Silent Spring* and worldwide environmental activism. Many more recent summaries of the pesticide situation repeat the same conclusions.

Throughout her work on *Silent Spring*, Carson had suffered from what she called "a catalogue of illnesses,"[59] viral and staph infections, arthritis, sinus trouble, iritis, and an ulcer. As a child, she had had scarlet fever and had often been absent from school because of illness, although her mother also kept her home whenever there was any kind of epidemic. She continued to be frequently ill.

There was considerable illness in Rachel Carson's family as well. Although her mother lived until she was nearly ninety, she had severe arthritis, as did Carson's father, who had suddenly collapsed and died twenty-

NORTHGATE HIGH SCHOOL LIBRARY

three years before the death of his wife. Carson's niece Marjorie also had arthritis, as well as severe diabetes, although she died of pneumonia.

Late in 1960, Carson found that even though she had asked directly, she had not been told the truth about a growth removed from her breast the previous spring. It had been malignant.

She flew to Cleveland for a consultation with Dr. George Crile, Jr., an expert she had consulted while doing her research for *Silent Spring*. Then she began radiation treatments, telling only her immediate family and close friends what was really wrong with her. "I want to do what must be done, but no more," she wrote to Dr. Crile. "After all, I still have several books to write, and can't spend the rest of my life in hospitals!!"[60] But a heart attack made her almost an invalid during her last year.

She never fully recovered from her last operation, a radioactive implant, dying some months later on 14 April 1964. Her friend Shirley Briggs comments that no one expected her to die so quickly,[61] but Carson's letters show that she herself suspected the summer of 1963 might be her last.

Carson received many honors during the brief period she lived after the publication of *Silent Spring*. Particularly meaningful to her was the Schweitzer Medal of the Animal Welfare Institute, since Albert Schweitzer's concept of "reverence for life" was a central focus of her own philosophy.

Even during this hectic period, Carson worked in a new area, the protection of animals, writing a strong foreword for Ruth Harrison's book *Animal Machines* (1964), which attacked the cruelty of newly intensified British methods of raising animals. She also joined the board of directors of the Defenders of Wildlife. "Until we have the courage to recognize cruelty for what it is—whether its victim is human or animal—" she had written earlier, "we cannot expect things to be much better in this world."[62]

The many memorials to Rachel Carson testify to the important causes she supported. When her correspondence swelled, after *Silent Spring*, with requests for information and assistance related to pesticide questions, she and a group of friends discussed the possibilities of an organization to answer such requests and keep the public informed on new developments, a task well beyond the powers of any one person. After her death, friends formed the Rachel Carson Trust for the Living Environment, now the Rachel Carson Council, to fulfill these goals.

"One of my keen interests," Carson wrote in 1951, "is the preservation of some natural seashore areas." "There are few beaches left that show no scarring traces of man's presence."[63] She herself willed funds to the Sierra Club and the Nature Conservancy to preserve some of these areas. On the fifth anniversary of Carson's death, journalist Ann Cottrell Free asked the public to demand that the government designate a fitting memorial to Rachel Carson. In response to the resulting public clamor, a series of coastal marshes in Maine was designated the Rachel Carson National Wildlife Refuge. Carson's childhood home in Springdale, Pennsylvania, now listed on the National Register of Historic Places, has become an ecological center and museum.

Many things have been named after Carson, among them a nature trail in Pennsylvania; schools in Montgomery County, Maryland, and New York City; research cruisers of the National Marine Fisheries Service and the University of California; and even a peregrine falcon, raised on the roof of the Interior Department building in Washington, in 1979, in an attempt to bring these endangered birds back to our nation's capital. Carson now appears, like other eminent Americans, on a postage stamp.

Perhaps most significant among recent honors is the Presidential Medal of Freedom, the highest award possible for a civilian recipient, presented posthumously to Rachel Carson on 9 June 1980 by President Jimmy Carter. Her adopted son, Roger Christie, accepted the medal. The citation reflects the range of her public accomplishments.

Never silent herself in the face of destructive trends, Rachel Carson fed a spring of awareness across America and beyond. A biologist with a gentle, clear voice, she welcomed her audiences to her love of the sea, while with an equally clear determined voice she warned Americans of the dangers human beings themselves pose for their own environment. Always concerned, always eloquent, she created a tide of environmental consciousness that has not ebbed.[64]

3

Lives in the Sea: *Under the Sea-Wind*

Despite the greater fame of her later books, a reader new to Rachel Carson should begin with *Under the Sea-Wind: A Naturalist's Picture of Ocean Life* (1941). With a rigorous scientific accuracy and thoroughness undiminished by the poetry of word pictures and building rhythms, Carson weaves three interlocking narratives portraying the life of the waters near the shore, the open sea, and the sea bottom. She unites form, content, and style to make this her most successful literary work.

In her foreword (not reprinted in the more readily available 1952 edition), Carson wrote that she wanted "to make the sea and its life as vivid a reality for those who may read the book as it has become for me." With flair and beauty, she creates a lively account culminating in a single effect, an ecological sense of the interdependence of all life.

Each narrative has its own focus. The main protagonists of Book I are two migrating birds, Blackfoot, leader of the sanderling flock, and his mate Silverbar, a yearling returning for the first time to the Arctic where she was born.

We meet them on an island in the Carolinas, a stopover on their trip north. When they reach the Arctic, they suffer an unusually severe spring snowstorm that takes many lives, before they can breed and raise their young during the brief northern summer. Then, as the season changes, they begin the long flight south. We leave them when they again reach the Carolinas, but they will travel deep into South America without us, before reaching their winter destination.

We share the adventures of other characters as well, fishing with Rynchops, the black skimmer, whose bill efficiently plows the water, suffering the tortures of a gill net with captured shad, and watching from the shore as fishermen drag a huge net to catch migrating mullet passing through the inlet. The story of Ookpik and his mate, white owls who must abandon their egg-filled nest during the great snow, is a tiny tragic vignette equal to many a short story of love and death.

Book II's endearing hero is Scomber the mackerel, who rushes from one breathtaking escape from death to the next. His picaresque adventures illustrate the dangers of sea life, where creatures must feed on one another for survival. Newborn, Scomber is the prey even of tiny shellfish and anchovies, but as he grows, his predators become more awesome, a six-foot rock cod lurking on an undersea ledge, a conger eel who chases Scomber through the water, and most dangerous of all, the nets of man.

Scomber is often saved only because his attackers are in turn attacked. Bluefish scatter the anchovies, while an inquisitive sea trout bites a comb jelly that has fastened Scomber in its sticky tentacles. When Scomber is already in the harvest of fish filling the nets of a mackerel seiner, razor-teethed dogfish slash holes in the nets to capture the trapped mackerel themselves. In the "indescribable confusion, in which the space circumscribed by the cork line became . . . a maelstrom of leaping fish, of biting teeth, of flashing green and silver," Scomber escapes, moving on to his winter home in "the deep, quiet waters along the edge of the continental shelf."

Book III focuses on Anguilla the eel, who ends ten years of maturation in an inland pond with her dramatic two-hundred-mile journey to the sea. Because little is known of the eels' pathways in the ocean, Book III's central chapter follows migrating sea trout, reminding us that "eels must have passed this way," but the final chapter returns us to the eels, already far out at sea.

Mingling there with European eels who have come from the other side of the ocean, the old eels die, leaving new larvae to trace once more the life history of the eel. By that autumn, hundreds of thousands of young eels have reached "the mouth of the bay from which, little more than a year before, Anguilla and her companions had set out for the deep sea."

Readers of *Under the Sea-Wind* may be surprised that Carson can make us care so much about the survival of a mackerel, whom at other times we might have fished for ourselves. Our allegiances are particularly jolted when Scomber comes "upon an unfamiliar object" diffusing a fishlike taste into the water. This turns out to be herring "bound to a large steel hook." To our relief, Scomber noses at it, but is not caught.

In my reading, I paused to consider how different the ocean would seem on my next visit—I wanted that to be as soon as possible—and how much I was learning through this effortless skimming of the pages. But Carson's narrative pulls the reader back, drawing one into the lives of Scomber the mackerel, Cynoscion the sea trout, and the other characters.

Carson's skill in handling action is evident throughout the book, in small incidents as well as the great chase scenes that often provide the dramatic climax for a chapter. The sanderling Silverbar's agile movements at the edge of the beach bring to life for us a small yet revealing bit of sea life. "She gauged the speed of the mound of water as it ran, toppling, up the beach. . . . Running under the very crest of the green water hill, Silverbar probed vigorously in the wet sand with opened bill and drew out the crab. Before the water could so much as wet her legs she turned and fled up the beach."

A longer segment dramatically portrays an eagle's attempts to steal an osprey's catch, while in another of Carson's beautifully orchestrated hunting scenes, tuna attack the school of mackerel. A five-hundred-pound tuna grazes Scomber's flank as it eats the fish next to him. Twice he barely misses the huge jaws, but he is saved when killer whales suddenly attack the tuna.

Specific details and precise use of language light up these scenes. In this one, "Scomber climbed up and up. The water was paling as it thinned away above them. Scomber could feel the thudding water vibration of an enormous fish climbing behind him, faster than a small mackerel could climb." As the action becomes more intense, the pace of the writing quickens.

"Spring Flight" is a clear example of Carson's deliberate control of time flow. Following the sanderlings from their arrival on the North Carolina barrier island until they leave to continue their northern migration, it describes their interrelationships with other migrating birds, native creatures, and unusual predators brought in by a severe storm.

At the beginning of the chapter, Carson dwells on the incidents of each instant of the tide, but as patterns are established, the time flow becomes faster. The chapter ends with a panoramic sweep: "As the earth rolled from darkness toward light, birds from many feeding places along the coast were hurrying along the flyways that lead to the north. . . . About an hour before dawn the sanderling flock . . . set out toward the north."

Carson carefully controls point of view as well. As the book opens, we sense a human eye, rather than a more cooly objective camera, filtering the action. This unseen narrator becomes omniscient observer when Carson wants us to get inside a bird, fish, or human protagonist to see and feel as they do. "Before the last shimmer of gold had faded from the surface," we read,

"Scomber's flanks began to tingle with quick, light vibrations as the water filled with a shoal of clamworms."

"Seine Haul," the highly dramatic finale to Scomber the mackerel's first year of life, interweaves points of view with the most complexity. The observing eye is dominant ("That night the sea burned with unusual phosphorescence"), but there are significant shifts to Scomber ("This was a larger school [of older mackerel] than Scomber had ever known before"), and a brief movement to birds resting on the sea who are almost struck by the cruising fishing vessel. The most unusual shift is to the fishermen on the mackerel boat.

After returning to the "nervous and uneasy" school of mackerel, Carson unifies her different points of view in the consciousness of a particularly imaginative young fisherman, not at sea long enough "to forget, if he ever would, the wonder, the unslakable curiosity he had brought to his job—curiosity about what lay under the surface." His is the only individual human point of view Carson uses.

When he has "time to think such thoughts," he wonders what the eyes of the mackerel have seen. Almost despite himself, he imagines the mackerel about to sound, or dive down to escape, before the net has closed beneath them. When they do sound, it is only after "their hour's heavy work wasted" that he realizes "what it meant [to him as a fisherman] that the mackerel had sounded."

As the chapter ends, one solitary vessel is trying to offset its bad luck of the night. The observing eye remains above the water with the boat, maintaining total objectivity, but Carson's careful manipulation of previous points of view has fastened our sympathies totally to the mackerel. After the attacking dogfish tear holes in the net, letting most of the mackerel pour through, the narrator quietly concludes with a view of Scomber, "directed by overmastering instinct . . . traveling far below the surface . . . to a place he himself had never known," the spawning grounds of the mackerel.

This scene may suggest that Carson takes a position against fishing and other human uses of the sea's resources, but the overall thrust of *Under the Sea-Wind* supports a philosophy of ecological balance, in which human needs are part of the total picture, as long as they are pursued with appropriate restraint.

Details of setting have two roles in *Under the Sea-Wind*. They supply factual information and help to create a feeling of immediacy. As the book opens, "Flood Tide" gives us not a general description of a southern Atlantic shore, but a specific picture of an island off the North Carolina coast on a particular spring night. Place, time, and atmospheric conditions help shape the content of the narrative, as Carson follows only creatures and events on this island during this nighttime flood tide, giving the chapter tight unity.

Since *Under the Sea-Wind* is a narrative, choosing appropriate protagonists was important. Carson felt the sea itself would be her "central character." She explains in the foreword that "no single animal . . . could live in all the various parts of the sea I proposed to describe. . . . The sense of the sea, holding the power of life and death over every one of its creatures from the smallest to the largest, would inevitably pervade every page."

Each book, however, has its own major characters, named and individualized in the manner of Henry Williamson, an English nature writer whose influence she acknowledged.[1] Where possible she uses scientific names, but, "Where that name is too formidable," she tells us in the foreword, "I have substituted something descriptive of the appearance of the creature, or, in the case of some of the Arctic animals, have used the Eskimo names." Scomber is the scientific name for the mackerel. The sanderlings' names are descriptive, while Ookpik is Eskimo.

Carson wants us to "project ourselves vicariously into" marine life. This means abandoning many human concepts, she explains, measuring time not by clock or calendar, but by light and darkness and the tides.

She believes that other creatures' lives will seem real to us, however, only when we relate them to our own, moving from our own feelings and reactions to empathy with theirs. In unskillful hands this can lead to what many critics call the "sin of anthropomorphism," seeing animals in human terms or imputing to them specifically human emotions and intelligence. Carson restricts herself to "analogy with human conduct" so that sea creatures will seem as real to us as they actually are.

She consciously distinguishes her approach from formal scientific writing. As she explains in the foreword:

I have spoken of a fish "fearing" his enemies . . . not because I suppose a fish experiences fear in the same way that we do, but because I think he *behaves as though he were frightened*. With the fish, the response is primarily physical; with us, primarily psychological. Yet if the behavior of the fish is to be understandable to us, we must describe it in the words that most properly belong to human psychological states.

When Carson writes that young shad dimly remember the river where they were born, she defines her concept of animal memory as a "heightened response of the senses as the delicate gills and the sensitive lateral lines perceived the lessening saltiness of the water and the changing rhythms and vibrations." The response is intuitive: physiological reactions influence action.

Joy and delight are human responses Carson often finds appropriate to describe the activities of birds. Rynchops, the black skimmer, takes "joy in flight and soaring motion," while mockingbirds produce "rippling, chuckling songs to charm their mates and delight themselves."

Her technique is most effective with Scomber the mackerel. When he is almost eaten by a comb jelly, we can share his sense of being "half dead with pain and exhaustion." We too would crawl into the nearest mass of seaweed to rest. In the most finely tuned example of her technique, Carson shows Scomber repeatedly leaping out of the water in frenzied attempts to escape the jaws of a tuna, each time "falling back with the heaviness of exhaustion." Here she does not specifically attribute the feeling to Scomber, but gives us an appropriate analogy to imagine ourselves in his place.

Scientists who want to transmit only proven factual knowledge often deplore the tendency of nonscientists writing about nature to treat animals as if they were human. Joseph Wood Krutch, an essayist who wrote many books about nature, believed that scientists should not ridicule "anthropomorphic" attitudes, contending that an exclusively mechanistic interpretation of animal behavior is equally misleading.[2]

As a biologist writing for the lay public, Carson wants neither to include anything unacceptable to scientists, nor to give the public inaccurate information. Thus she avoids both extreme anthropomorphism and the mechanistic approach. Like Henry Williamson in *Tarka the Otter*, she wanted to enter into a character's life, see "with its eyes," and follow and portray "the moving drama of its everyday life."[3]

Under the Sea-Wind gracefully fulfills the traditional goals of literature, to simultaneously teach and delight. This brief book contains a remarkable amount of information, as Carson weaves her facts into the unfolding of character and the narratives of action. A glossary at the end provides additional factual material. There we can learn which names are scientific, or what creature is related to another. Although the glossary is extensive for the size of the book, its scope is limited, so that the curious reader may need to seek other sources to learn more.

Carson has many techniques of unobtrusively introducing information. As she describes the skimmer's fishing technique, for example, we learn why its bill is called a "cutwater." Deft images add details as, "with a flashing of the white wing bars that distinguished them from other sandpipers," or, "and shrimp swam with backward flipping of their tails."

The sea's food chains are dramatized rather than explained. In one of the many circular eating scenes, a ghost crab eating beach fleas is alarmed by birds who were themselves alarmed by a fisherman. The crab flees into the sea, where it is eaten by a channel bass who is later attacked by a shark. The remains of the bass eventually reach the sand, where they are eaten by beach fleas.

Carson swiftly yet clearly presents complex background information. Describing the dangers to the newborn Scomber, she presents the whole interrelated ecological community of this part of the ocean. As the eels descend to the sea, they pass a high clay cliff. She pauses briefly to trace its geological history through examining its physical details.

When particular sex roles differ from the usual, Carson notes the facts, as she would any other information: "Then the cock phalarope took charge of the nest, to sit for eighteen days, warming the eggs to life." In the next paragraph, the male knot flies above "his small dappled mate who was brooding their four eggs in the nest far below." This juxtaposition makes us realize that either way is normal. As she notes in her foreword, "the reader is an observer of events which are narrated with little or no comment."

At times, we may wonder how Carson knows things reported so factually about places or occasions difficult to observe. She acknowledges some sources in the foreword, but our sense of her scientific accuracy is enhanced by the technique of careful qualification when there is insufficient basis for her statements. When swimming shrimp flexed their tails, she writes, "they could bring the hinder lights to bear on the water beyond and below them and so perhaps were better able to see the small copepods . . . they hunted."

Carson always explores the implications of her material, seeking the larger perspective, the pattern behind individual facts, and the larger pattern behind the smaller. She relates the tides, for example, to the movements of the sea onto the lands and back into their basins over long periods of geologic history.

Tides and the flights of shore birds, she tells us in the foreword, "are as nearly eternal" as any things in our earthly life can be. They existed before man, and "continue year in, year out, through the centuries and the ages, while man's kingdoms rise and fall." She clearly specifies their symbolic function in a later article, noting the "symbolic as well as actual beauty in the migration of the birds; in the ebb and flow of the tides. . . ."[4]

They are symbols not in the usual sense of things standing for concepts, but as particular, ephemeral activities providing knowable prototypes for "timeless" activities that have been repeated throughout the life of the earth. These cycles or rhythms give form to the work as a whole, as well as to individual books or chapters, and ultimately help express her overall philosophy of ecological interrelationships.

Each of the three books has an uneven number of chapters—five, seven, and three, respectively—with the central chapter providing a calm plateau at the height of the action. The lengths of the books place Book II, the story of the mackerel, in the preeminent position.

Books I and II run from spring to fall, but Book II expands the time scheme, beginning in April rather than June, and ending when it is almost winter. Book III begins in the fall, although there is a brief recapitulation of the spring ten years before when Anguilla the eel arrived at the river. Ending in March, Book III reverses the earlier spring-to-fall pattern, so that *Under the Sea-Wind* begins and ends in spring. This emphasizes Carson's insistence on the completeness and importance of natural cycles.

Carson carefully patterns her structure so that "Arctic Rendezvous" is not only central among the five chapters of Book I, but longest. This reinforces the importance of the activities it describes. Birds nest, and brood and raise their young, while plants flower and quickly form their seeds during the brief Arctic summer.

The remaining chapters of Book I are balanced pairs. The climactic episode of the first chapter is the netting of the migrating shad, passing through the sound on their way to the river to spawn. The fifth chapter describes the netting of the mullet who are making their fall migration through the inlet out into the open sea. Chapter 2 follows the spring migration of the birds from North Carolina to the Arctic, while chapter 4 describes their fall migration south.

The central chapter of Book II, "The Harbor," plays a role much like that of "Arctic Rendezvous" in the first book. Again it is summer, the time for growth. Scomber and other young mackerel come in from the sea for a quiet period of maturation. Although there are still dangers, food and shelter are ample. To remind us that life cycles overlap, with birth and death ever present, Carson counterbalances this quiescent period in Scomber's life with a dramatic account of the "fateful journey" of the moon jelly Aurelia, who are battered and destroyed, "but not until the larvae held within their arms had been liberated into the shallow waters. Thus the cycle came to the full."

When the noted oceanographer and writer, William Beebe, chose a portion of *Under the Sea-Wind* for his *Book of Naturalists*,[5] he combined the first and third chapters of Book III to form what he called "Odyssey of the Eel." In the middle chapter, "Winter Haven," Carson leaves the eels to follow other fish seeking shelter in the deep, warm waters of the abyss. She surmises that the eels too must have passed here.

Book II, then, is the most integrated of the narratives in coherence of form, characterization, and viewpoint. With its emphasis on individual variations within a fixed general pattern, Scomber's story becomes the prototypical life cycle of *Under the Sea-Wind*. Reviewing the book when it first came out, Beebe had commented: "The author is at her best in her complete life histories. There, her attention is concentrated upon a single individual organism, about which environment, experiences and enemies, are made to revolve, and on which they focus."[6]

Carson tells us that *Under the Sea-Wind* moves from the shore areas to the continental slope to the deep waters of the abyss. Book I stays with its migrating protagonists near the "Edge of the Sea," as its title indicates, but the other two books range through the limits of their characters' migrations. The mackerel move from the continental slope to the harbor and then out to sea again, while the eels travel downriver, far out into the abyss and then once more to the mouth of the river. Each of the books traces a larger circle, encompassing a greater portion of the sea.

Rachel Carson was a slow and painstaking writer, drafting revision after revision until she was satisfied. Among her manuscripts, one finds seven successive drafts of a single page, the beginning of "Spring Flight." There is only one exception to the many heavily corrected manuscripts for each chapter. One eight-page handwritten manuscript, apparently a first draft, was incorporated into chapter 13 almost completely unchanged.

As we read *Under the Sea-Wind*, form and style seem to be a flowing, seamless whole. There is always a sense of orderly development but the formal structure never seems obvious or overlaid on the material. It takes close inspection to reveal the intricacies of Carson's style as well, although such techniques as alliteration may be immediately noticeable.

Many of her rhetorical devices are those we associate with poetry: alliteration, assonance, and other sound echoes; rhythmic patterns; images utilizing multiple senses and abundant color; phrases used as motifs; and metaphors and similes.

The opening paragraphs of the book show Carson's use of alliteration to create atmosphere. *S*'s predominate, often associated with breathy *w*'s to simulate the hush of evening settling over island and water: "on its western shore the wet sand" is followed later by "sheen of silver" and "score of wing beats."

Carson also creates epithetlike descriptions through alliteration, identifying a rat with the phrase "crafty with the cunning of years." Assonance frequently accompanies alliteration, as in the *e* sounds of "western" and "wet," or may be used with other sound echoes as in "bits of sticks" with its combination of percussive consonants. She never allows these techniques to make her writing uncomfortably lush. During one of the episodes where creatures in turn attack and eat others, the alliteration accumulates, only to be neatly undercut by a spare statement describing the climactic act of the series: "the blue heron . . . came upon the rat and speared him."

She often incorporates both grammatical and rhythmic parallels within her sentence structure to build momentum and effect. In a brief example within a larger unit, we read, "The sound was the stirring of many wings, the passage of many feathered bodies through the low vegetation of the plain, the murmur of myriad bird voices." When using techniques like these, her writing resembles Walt Whitman's poetry.

Multiple sense images help create immediacy and involvement for the reader. When shad are caught in the gill net, we feel the "burning, choking collar." Our sense of touch responds when we read that a "wave of motion stroked the tops of the grasses." We see rocky stream beds "grooved in the hill," while "the brackish water of a shallow bay" calls on our sense of taste, and the rattle of dead seed heads on our sense of hearing.

Carson spreads color freely in her descriptions of the horizontal communities layered in deep sea waters and her reports of how creatures take on camouflage to blend with their surroundings. Her vivid palette adds intensity to dramas such as Ookpik the white owl's capture of a ptarmigan, which he spots by "the moving balls of shining black" that were its eyes. The dominant color of the scene is the white of the Arctic.

The white foe moved nearer, blending into the pale sky; the white prey moved, unfrightened, over the snow. There was a soft whoosh of wings—a scattering of feathers—and on the snow a red stain spread, red as a new-laid ptarmigan egg before the shell pigments have dried.

Both phrases and themes sometimes become motifs that Carson repeats within chapters for unity and occasionally uses as bridges between chapters. In both "Spring Flight" and the parallel chapter "Summer's End," we find the phrase "point of land called ship's shoal," while references to the "bay shaped like a leaping porpoise" help unify the action of "Arctic Rendezvous." Migration is a frequent thematic motif, used specifically to link the first and third chapters of Book III.

Similes and metaphors enhance Carson's vivid pictures, helping us visualize things we have never seen, like the multitudes of newborn crustaceans described as "clouds of goblin-headed young." They also provide occasional links between sections, as when the metaphor "thin shell of the new moon" echoes the previous paragraph where the water was turning over the shells on the sand.

The most important role of similes and metaphors is to help establish the interrelationships basic to Carson's ecological world view. When she writes that "marsh grasses waded boldly out into dark water," we see both the grasses and the long-legged birds implied by the metaphor as living parts of an interdependent community.

The relationship reflected most often in Carson's imagery is that of the land and the sea. The skimmer's bill "plowed a miniature furrow" as it cut the water. There are "caravans" of mackerel and eels and "meadows" of hydroids (plantlike animals), while in an extended comparison, prawns and crabs "start up and dart away before the rooting snout of a fish, like a rabbit before a hound."

The shifting borders of land and sea are evident from the beginning of the book—"it was hard to say where water ended and land began"—but the sea always seems dominant. The final paragraphs make the relationship explicit: "And as the eels lay offshore . . . waiting for the time when they should enter the waters of the land, the sea, too, lay restless, awaiting the time when once more it should encroach upon the coastal plain, and creep up the sides of the foothills, and lap at the bases of the mountain ranges" so that once again "the places of its cities and towns would belong to the sea."

This is part of the broad perspective in time and space Carson brings to all she portrays, so that we too will see ourselves as a small part of the total picture, as dependent as any other creatures on the environment around us, and living in "a moment of geologic time."

Man is the one wanton destroyer in *Under the Sea-Wind*. Although this theme is far less prominent than in Carson's later work, we see him disturbing natural cycles and balances as he captures huge numbers of the fish attempting to swim upriver to spawn, or kills merely for sport.

When golden plovers leave the Arctic in "the greatest flight of many years," the old priest, Father Nicollet, remembers "the great flights he had seen in his youth, before the gunners had thinned the plover flights to a remnant of their former size." Commenting that some of these birds will not complete the flight, Carson mentions those that will "be picked off by gunners, defying the law for . . . fancied pleasure." She describes only one nonhuman instance of unnecessary killing, when porpoises kill a few mackerel "in sport," but do not follow the school because they already have gorged on other fish.

She makes her points through unstated lessons—when for example, a fox does not dig into a lemming burrow he has discovered because he has just killed and eaten a ptarmigan—as well as direct comments. When Ookpik's mate must leave her eggs to save her own life, Carson notes the greater chance for survival of all the Arctic creatures the "owls-to-be" might have eaten. There is never a sentimental objection to killing. Telling us that of one hundred thousand eggs, only one or two shad will return to spawn, she comments that "by such ruthless selection the species are kept in check."

She emphasizes repeatedly that in nature, nothing is wasted. After the netting of the mullet, small fish thrown out on the beach are eaten first by gulls, then by fish crows and ghost crabs, and finally, to dispose of the last remnants, by the sand hoppers. "For in the sea," she writes, "nothing is lost. One dies, another lives, as the precious elements of life are passed on and on in endless chains."

Animals participate in these cycles intuitively. Human beings, Carson implies, have lost their intuitive respect for natural elements, and in their conscious acts, all too often waste or destroy them.

Although the book is made up of three stories, it is considered a nonfictional account of the life of the sea, as Carson intended it. The fictional approach lets her painlessly transmit both her information and her attitude of love and respect for all life.

As a gifted writer who had written short stories from childhood through her college years, Carson used the form with surety and finesse, fulfilling all the demands of classic realistic writing. Henry James and William Dean Howells, both practitioners and theorists of American realism when it first separated from romanticism in the nineteenth century, described its basic requirements: everyday subjects; common, understandable language; a close relationship of character and action with action flowing from character and character influencing action; and no inappropriate "happy endings."

Above all, they believed overt moralism or didacticism should be avoided, with any lessons or moral purpose inherent in the treatment of the material. Carson's use of the intelligent observer, filtering what is seen through a fine consciousness and sensibility, also accords with Henry James's theory and practice.

Like all good fiction, *Under the Sea-Wind* provides a heightened version of ordinary life. In hunting scenes that demonstrate the economy of nature, every creature who might possibly participate, does, so that the cycles are complete.

Rachel Carson admitted her own fondness for *Under the Sea-Wind*. "It has many faults," she commented later, "some of which greater knowledge and maturity may have corrected, but I doubt that a writer ever quite recaptures the freshness of a first book."[7] The glowing reviews, both in 1941 and 1952, found few faults. Beebe complained that the density of facts made the book difficult to read aloud, but he was "unable to detect a single error."[8] A more recent critic noted only that Carson diminishes the effect of words used in unusual ways by repeating them too soon.[9]

Chapters appear in anthologies of nature writing and of sea writing. Although some editors prefer her better known and more factual *The Sea Around Us*, A. C. Spectorsky, editor of *The Book of the Sea*, calls the earlier book "more personal, more closely integrated and, in the opinion of some, a more careful and thoughtful work."[10]

Because of its tremendous impact on public knowledge and attitudes, *Silent Spring* is Rachel Carson's most important book, but *Under the Sea-Wind* is a frequent favorite—of Carson's colleague and friend, Dorothy Algire, of Judge Curtis Bok, another friend and a gifted author himself, of Brian Vesey-Fitzgerald, the editor of the British one-volume edition of the three sea books,[11] and of mine. In *Under the Sea-Wind*, Carson's gifts as a writer and as a scientist most perfectly come together.

4

~·

Return to Oceanus: *The Sea Around Us*

In ancient times, some believed that Oceanus, the unknown sea, was a place of "unattainable continents or of
beautiful islands in the distant ocean." Others feared the
"bottomless gulf at the edge of the world," "a dark world
from which there was no return" encircling the known
earth with menace and chaos. Portraits of strange creatures from that imagined world, and of courageous ships
that sailed out to explore it, embellish the front end papers of *The Sea Around Us*, balanced at the rear of the
book by portions of old maps that tried to impose order
on the forbidding chaos.

These pictures are the keys to Carson's intentions
in her second book. Explorers had tracked most of the
sea's surface and had just begun to plumb its depths.
Carson wanted to gather the results of these explorations
and with simplicity and clarity create the comprehensive
book she had wished for as a child fascinated by an ocean
she had never seen. It would be not only a book for those
who knew nothing about the sea, but one scientists would
not quarrel with and might even find a source of fresh
insights.[1]

Carson collected "an immense amount" of material.
"More than once," she wrote after publication, "I asked
myself why I had ever undertaken such an unending
task." But more than just research went into *The Sea
Around Us*. "In a sense," she explained, "I have been col-

47

lecting material for this ocean book all my life— . . . my mind has stored up everything I have ever learned about it as well as my own thoughts, impressions, and emotions."[2] As a result, she imbues her facts with an enthusiastic respect for the natural world's marvelous system of ecological interrelationships, and with her awe and love for all life.

For Carson, content always determines form. The three-part division follows a logical progression, with "Mother Sea," the first and major portion, covering the sea itself. Eight chapters describe the formation of the oceans and ocean life, the nature of the sea, and the changing relationships between land and ocean.

Balanced against Part I are Parts II and III, with three chapters each. "The Restless Sea" covers the forces which act on the oceans—winds, moon and sun, and the rotation of the earth—while "Man and the Sea about Him" shows how the oceans affect human life, completing the implications of the title, "The Sea Around Us." The book closes with an extensive annotated list of "Suggestions for Further Reading."

Careful logic orders the parts as well as the whole. Within its historical framework, Part I follows a downward course through the ocean. First an introductory chapter, "The Gray Beginnings," tells "how the young planet Earth acquired an ocean, . . . a story pieced together from many sources and containing whole chapters the details of which we can only imagine." In Carson's unfolding drama, we see mountains thrust up and worn away as seas repeatedly rise up over the land and fall back again. The first living cell appears, ultimately developing into "a race of creatures" that can be transformed "into beings with the body and brain and the mystical spirit of man."

There is a "Chart of the History of the Earth and Its Life" to graphically clarify the chronology of mountains, volcanoes, glaciers, and the development of different forms of life.

The next five chapters explore the sea from top to bottom. In "The Pattern of the Surface," we learn about the surprisingly abundant life of deceptively barren looking waters, and how the forms of this life vary with the environment. "The Changing Year" follows the changes in marine life through the seasons.

In "The Sunless Sea," we descend into the "miles-deep," "least known region of the sea" that covers "about half the earth." Tracing the discoveries made by both divers and modern instruments, Carson shows us strange creatures adapted to immense pressures and total darkness in waters formerly thought unable to sustain life.

Chapter 5 guides us through the "Hidden Lands" of the abyss found at the bottom of each great ocean, filled with huge mountains and canyons. Carson explores forces that might have created them, and then details historical facts that could have led to the legend of the lost continent of Atlantis. She ends with the true story of the Dogger Bank, a modern lost land now a productive fishing ground.

"The Long Snowfall" stays at the bottom of the ocean. Carson describes the sediments covering the ocean floor, final remains of all that return to the sea, as if they were the flakes of a great snowfall. Deep in the red clay of the North Pacific, in a "zone of immense pressures and glacial cold," she tells us, there are even "sharks' teeth and the ear bones of whales." "Even now, in our own lifetime," Carson closes, continuing her striking image, "the flakes of a new snow storm are falling, falling, one by one, out there on the ocean floor. . . . Who will read their record, ten thousand years from now?"

"The Birth of an Island" returns us to the surface, then gradually takes us lower and lower into the ocean, recapitulating the downward movement of Part I. Carson relates the history of volcanic islands, those bits of land in the middle of the ocean that rise abruptly from the waves, then slowly wear down, if they are not blasted away, until they are once more part of the sea.

In "The Shape of Ancient Seas," the final chapter in Part I, Carson shows that our age is one of rising seas. Then she goes back to early geologic time to trace the oceans' repeated invasions of the land, suggesting that at some time in history, every part of North America has probably been under a shallow sea. Her return to the seas' beginnings links this chapter with the opening chapter, "The Gray Beginnings," completing the circular structure of Part I.

Each of the chapters of Part II focuses on one of the forces that creates movements in the sea in the form of waves, currents, and tides. Carson explores both our growing knowledge of how these forces work, and our attempts to put the movements to use. Again the chapters carry us downward into the sea, treating first waves on the surface, then currents in shallow waters, followed by those deep below the surface, and finally the tides that encompass all the waters.

The last chapter in Part II ends with fascinating examples of marine creatures so finely attuned to their environment that they time such activities as spawning to coincide precisely with specific points in the tidal cycle.

Part III opens with "The Global Thermostat," a discussion of the role of currents in determining climate. Carson covers both familiar surface currents like the Gulf Stream, and the less known systems of currents deep beneath the sea. Using evidence from both historical records and folklore, she tests theories of weather variation, emphasizing a recent explanation that posits two-thousand-year cycles linked to the actions of deep currents, with less extreme shorter cycles within them. After demonstrating that the theory is feasible, she suggests possible implications for the present time.

"Wealth from the Salt Seas" covers the mineral resources of the oceans, their formation and locations, how sea creatures use them, and our attempts to extract them. Again the movement is downward from the surface to resources at the bottom of the oceans.

In her final chapter, "The Encircling Sea," Carson again brings us back to beginnings, completing yet another circle encompassing the entire book. This time she traces human exploration of the seas, beginning with the Phoenicians. Exploring ancient theories and myths about the sea, she shows how they were gradually disproven, then relates the history of navigational charts and instruments. She includes an appreciative discussion of the literary merits of the pamphlets on sailing directions and coast pilots, issued by all the maritime nations of the world. "In these writings of the sea," she tells us, "there is a pleasing blend of modernity and antiquity," just as there is, we might add, in *The Sea Around Us*.

With exposition of facts her primary goal, and a desire to appeal both to scientists and laymen, Carson had to seek accuracy and utmost clarity, as well as techniques to intrigue the reader. Her research was exhaustive. She consulted over a thousand sources and conferred or corresponded with experts all over the world. One or more of a long list of consultants evaluated individual chapters before publication.

Carson does not simply present information, but systematically evaluates it, distinguishing among three categories of facts: historical material; theories supported by enough evidence to be generally accepted; and open or partially answered questions. "In spite of theories to the contrary," she writes, "the weight of geologic evidence seems to be that the locations of the major ocean basins and the major continental land masses are today much the same as they have been since a very early period of the earth's history."

In chapter 4 she mentions a mysterious layer hanging between the surface and the ocean bottom, discovered by echo-sounding devices. Using underwater cameras and recorders scientists were trying to identify it. After presenting evidence obtained so far, Carson concludes that "the sea's phantom bottom may consist of small planktonic shrimps, of fishes, or of squids," but "no one is sure . . . although the discovery may be made any day." Ten years later in the revised editon, she notes that "the mystery of the scattering layer has not been completely resolved," and "in all probability," there will be different explanations for different areas of the ocean.

"The Long Snowfall" shows Carson's talent at presenting a sweeping yet accurate overview. Discussing whether the rocky floor of the Atlantic may have sagged under the terrific weight of its sediments, she reviews the various theories, including just enough specifics to explain them without interrupting the flow and balance of her exposition.

She never simplifies to the point of hiding underlying complexities. "The Shape of Ancient Seas" explains the various causes of the sea's inroads on the land so that we understand them, yet still wonder at "These grander tides of earth, whose stages are measurable not in hours but in millennia."

Carson's manuscripts reflect her efforts to reach the nonscientists among her readers. In a draft of the chapter on "Surface Waters" that became chapters 2 and 3, she underlined the word *diatom*, and noted, "explain."[3] Explanations and scientific terms generally are clear, but there are occasional exceptions. The word *pelagic* appears several times, but is defined as "free-swimming" only on its second use. *Sessile* is used without explanation, although readers may realize from its application to clams and mussels that its meaning is "permanently attached," the opposite of *pelagic*.

Carson varies her rhetorical techniques to maintain interest, moving rapidly from general statements to specific examples, and often stressing the unusual. Describing how different forms of life developed in the sea, she introduces sponges, jellyfish and "curiously fruiting seaweeds." There are particularly descriptive details, as in the picture of "gooseberry-like comb jellies, armed with grasping tentacles." She spreads her net widely to enhance her facts, including such sidelights as the Greek derivation of the word *plankton*, meaning "wandering," and sharpens our perception of the normal with dramatic exceptions. The vegetation of the Sargasso Sea, for example, is so thick that there were legends of ships trapped in the weeds.

Comparisons are an effective tool. Relating oceanographic research to space research, she writes that "knowledge of undersea topography lagged considerably behind our acquaintance with the landscape of the near side of the moon." She conveys a sense of the size of undersea mountain ranges by letting us know they are twice as wide as the Andes. Getting into homier examples, she tells us that "By midsummer the large red jellyfish Cyanea may have grown from the size of a thimble to that of an umbrella."

Carson often introduces a question she can answer or a theory she can debate to enhance the liveliness of the text. Exciting dramatizations perform the same purpose, as in her portrayal of the formation of the moon and oceans: "The new earth, freshly torn from its parent sun, was a ball of whirling gases, intensely hot, rushing through the black spaces of the universe on a path and at a speed controlled by immense forces." So her story begins.

Techniques of recapitulation and summary, often in

highly poetic form, reinforce the exposition. At the beginning of the book, Carson presents the three witnesses of the formation of the seas: rocks, moon, and stars. Each is introduced in a long phrase, then gracefully united with the others in a summary sentence at the end of the paragraph, which is also the thesis statement.

The keynotes of Carson's factual writing are precision and economy. Manuscripts show how carefully she edited out extraneous words and facts. The omission of irrelevant details prevents a cluttered text, but some readers may end up curious about the few unexplained matters, such as the location of the Eddystone Light, the site of one of her examples.

References from history and folklore deepen the perspective and add intriguing sidelights. In "The Changing Year," she describes the poisonous Gonyaulax, a minute phosphorescent plant which gives the water an ominous glow. It makes fish and shellfish that eat it toxic, so that they act on the human nervous system as strychnine does. The Indians, she tells us, understood its message, posting watchers to warn the unwary not to take food from such waters.

Reading about the sea's resources, we learn that ancient Greeks, Romans, and Egyptians perfected the solar evaporation of salt, using methods still practiced today. The Germans were less successful when they tried to extract gold from the sea to pay World War I debts. The cost of extraction, it turned out, was far greater than the value of the gold.

Quotations from direct observers, such as Thor Heyerdahl's description of squids jumping onto his raft, the *Kon-Tiki*, contribute freshness and immediacy. A rhyme sung by American airmen during World War II,

> If we don't find Ascension
> Our wives will get a pension,

adds both humor and a dramatic illustration of the isolation of volcanic islands in the South Atlantic.

The motif of exploration gives *The Sea Around Us* a cohesive narrative thread. This is particularly true in historically based chapters, but Carson also uses it to present scientific information, such as the topography of the ocean bottom. Giving us facts as part of the story of their discovery not only provides continuity, but lets us in on the excitement of following new developments.

Among Carson's rare inconsistencies is a confusing mixture of units used for measuring depth. She describes ice as fifteen feet thick and gives the depth of the Mariana Trench as 10,863 meters or about 6.7 miles, but reports a line breaking at fifteen hundred fathoms.

Carson always uses "man" for human beings as a group. This of course was common practice in 1951—sensitivities had not yet been raised—but when she moves from clearly all-male populations, like early explorers, to more modern groups, like researchers, the verbal implications that they too are all male can be disturbing.

Her association of the evolving race of men emerging from "mother sea" with "each of us" emerging from a mother's fluid-filled womb to begin "his" life we know refers to both men and women. But when we realize that all the experts mentioned and sources quoted in the book are male, we cannot be sure when her use of "man" is generic, and when it is merely descriptive.

When Carson accepted a National Book Award for *The Sea Around Us*, she said, "If there is poetry in my book about the sea, it is not because I deliberately put it there, but because no one could write truthfully about the sea and leave out the poetry."[4] Perhaps she did not consciously seek to make her writing poetic, but the comment seems disingenuous. Her editing shows clear concern for beauty as well as accuracy and clarity, with careful attention to images, rhythms, and sound.

Literary techniques enhance readability and support the transmission of information, but they do much more.

There is a contagious sense of excitement and discovery in Carson's writing, reflected in its glow of vitality, in its rhythmic buildups and intensifying cadences, and in the beauty of word pictures. She infects us with her own wonderful delight at the marvels, large and small, she is sharing with us.

Among her notes is a card with Joseph Conrad's comments in the introduction to his novel, *The Nigger of the "Narcissus"*, that the written word must appeal through the senses. Carson emphasizes sense impressions in her graphically described scenes. When she writes, "we begin to feel the mystery and the alien quality of the deep sea—the gathering darkness, the growing pressure, the starkness of a seascape," we can imagine that we are travelling with her along the steeper declivities of the continental slope.

Sounds dominate this passage from "The Changing Year": "the chorus of frogs rises again from the wet lands, the different sounds of the wind which stirs the young leaves where a month ago it rattled the bare branches." Sight and touch combine in the metaphor of "gorgeously plumed seaworms carpeting an underlying shoal."

Similes and metaphors are the most common images, with references to the land making the unknown sea seem more familiar. There are "beasts of the plankton" roaming through the water, while fish move over the plains of the abyss "like herds of cattle." She paints a dramatic scene when she describes summer luminescence, mainly from the protozoan Noctiluca, which causes "fishes, squids, or dolphins to fill the water with racing flames and to clothe themselves in a ghostly radiance."

"The Long Snowfall" depends on two interrelated metaphors, the "snowfall" itself, and the concept of "reading" the deposited sediments. When Carson declares that "the sediments are a sort of epic poem of the earth," she refers back to an image in the opening chapter, the idea that we can read the history "first inscribed on rock pages."

There is subtle personification in Carson's description of sleeping volcanoes and islands that "stand on the shoulders" of an undersea mountain chain. In "The Birth of an Island," she extends the personification of the title, writing of "little, stillborn islands" and "Krakatoa's dramatic passing."

She uses colors to evoke an emotional response but then explains them scientifically.

The deep blue water of the open sea far from land is the color of emptiness and barrenness; the green water of the coastal areas, with all its varying hues, is the color of life. The sea is blue because the sunlight is reflected back to our eyes from the water molecules or from very minute particles suspended in the sea. In the journey of the light rays downward into the water and back to our eyes, all the red rays of the spectrum and most of the yellow have been absorbed, so it is chiefly the cool, blue light that we see. Where the water is rich in plankton, it loses the glassy transparency that permits this deep penetration of the light rays. The yellow and brown and green hues of the coastal waters are derived from the minute algae and other micro-organisms so abundant there.

The rhythms of Carson's writing are most striking when they reflect the natural rhythms of her subjects. Describing tides in the molten earth, the movements of the words are broad and flowing. Writing about the effect of the seasons on surface waters, she mimics their movements: "The surface waters move with the tides, stir to the breath of the winds, and rise and fall to the endless, hurrying forms of the waves."

Rhythms sometimes unite with balancing grammatical repetitions in undulating phrases.

Fishes and plankton, whales and squids, birds and sea turtles, all are linked by unbreakable ties to certain kinds of water— to warm water or cold water, to clear or turbid water, to water rich in phosphates or in silicates.

Repeated vowels and consonants, assonance or alliteration, or more complicated textures of sound play, often add to the musical quality of Carson's writing and help to transmit what to her is an essential emotional response to the sea. Look at the interplay of sounds in these two basically factual sentences, especially the echoing *o*'s and the pattern of consonants:

Rocky ledges, shoals of sand or clay or rock, and coastal islands in the mouths of bays all play their part in the fate of the waves that advance toward shore. The long swells that roll from the open ocean toward the shores of northern New England seldom reach it in full strength.

Some passages are so rich in musical rhythms and sound structures that it is possible to lose the meaning in response to what some critics have called Carson's hypnotic prose, but in most cases, their judicious use adds immeasurably to the impact of the book.

Carson carefully controls point of view and tone. She begins the book with a clear *I* for herself, *you* for the reader, and a vaguer *we*, sometimes standing for all of us, sometimes for the scientific community. In one manuscript version of a passage about investigations of the ocean bottom, she changed all the *you*'s to *we*'s, presumably seeking closer identification between reader and writer.

She usually presents information from a neutral third-person point of view, interpolating refreshing first-person recollections or opinions, as in "the adjective I like best." Sometimes she specifically draws the reader into an experience, commenting that "Our minds are at once taken out from the earth," or suggesting, "If you visited this place and talked to the meteorologist in charge. . . ." She clearly expects reader participation to last beyond the reading of the book. "The next time you wonder why the water is so cold at certain coastal resorts, remember that . . . the Labrador Current is between you and the Gulf Stream."

In one passage there is an odd intrusion of the omniscient storyteller approach of *Under the Sea-Wind*. Describing moon jellies gathering in thousands, Carson writes, "and the birds see their pale forms shimmering deep down in the green water."

Her tone is usually cool and objective, but sometimes irrepressible spirits rise enthusiastically to the surface: "The unrelieved darkness of the deep waters has produced weird and incredible modifications of the abyssal fauna." Not afraid of words like *paradox* or *miracle*, she loves strange as well as ordinary examples. Occasionally awe-inviting words like *incredible* or *unthinkable* or *fascinating* come a bit too thickly.

Carson's rare touches of humor are dry, understated comments. Writing about the formation of the seas, she tells us, "it is not surprising that . . . explanations do not always agree. For the plain and inescapable truth is that no one was there to see." Commenting that northern fur seals probably do not feed on "commercially important fishes," she concludes, "Presumably four million seals could not compete with commercial fishermen for the same species without the fact being known."

The story of Falcon Island, "a physical bit of the British Empire in the Pacific," has an appropriately British tinge. The island disappeared in 1913 only to rise again thirteen years later, remaining in place until 1949. "Then it was reported by the Colonial Under Secretary to be missing again."

Like her references to history and myth, Carson's literary allusions add resonance and depth, but to the poetic rather than the expository aspects of her writing. She copied down pages of quotations about the ocean's awe-inspiring grandeur and timelessness, or its poetic aspects, in her notes, including Keats's belief that the earth's poetry is never dead, and Whittier's line that "Nature speaks in symbols and in sign." She uses a similarly transcendental quotation from Llewelyn Powys, "A deep and tremulous earth-poetry," to precede the sixth chapter.

Each chapter has a literary epigraph that introduces the topic, sets the tone, and sometimes even suggests the style. This is especially true of the quotation from Genesis that introduces "The Gray Beginnings": "And the earth was without form, and void; and darkness was upon the face of the deep."

Literary references sometimes contribute to Carson's system of interrelationships. We are reminded of the quotation from Milton that is chapter 3's epigraph when he reappears in a passage quoted from Charles Darwin. The poet Swinburne, known for his own lushly mellifluous writing filled with assonance and alliteration, links the second and third parts of the book, introducing both the last chapter of Part II and the first in Part I. Melville's words provide the epigraph for chapter 2, and the imagery of both surface-water chapters reflects his influence. Carson had noted in her manuscript that she should see Melville in relation to meadows.

When she recollects her own deep-sea voyage to introduce the chapter "Wind, Sun, and the Spinning of the Earth," she remembers that sunset in the fog "set us to searching our memories for quotations from Coleridge." Her sense of the sea's mysteries reflects his influence, as her chapter title, "The Sunless Sea," echoes Coleridge's poem "Kubla Khan."

Underlying and strengthening all of Carson's writing is her coherent philosophic base, implicit in presentations of facts and often explicit in summarizing comments. Her most important controlling theme is the concept of the earth as an ecologically balanced, interlocking whole where nothing is wasted.

Small vignettes bring the idea to life.

What happens to a diatom in the upper, sunlit strata of the sea may well determine what happens to a cod lying on a ledge of some rocky canyon a hundred fathoms below, . . . or to a prawn creeping over the soft oozes of the sea floor in the blackness of mile-deep water.

"Feeding directly on the diatoms and other groups of minute unicellular algae," she explains,

are the marine protozoa, many crustaceans, the young of crabs, barnacles, sea worms, and fishes. Hordes of the small carnivores, the first link in the chain of flesh eaters, move among these peaceful grazers. . . . From the plankton the food chains lead on . . .

An appreciative reviewer wrote exuberantly that "Everybody eats everybody, and Miss Carson enjoys and describes it all."[5]

Carson sees nature as parsimonious in the use of minerals as well. When the heavy, cold surface layers of water sink, in the spring, displacing warmer layers below, rich stores of minerals are brought up from the bottom of the continental shelf to be used once more. "Nothing is wasted in the sea," she states; "every particle of material is used over and over again, first by one creature, then by another."

Human beings participate as well. In her discussion of the continental shelf, she comments on the resources it offers: fish and seaweeds in shallow water above; and beneath it, petroleum.

The concepts of natural and historical cycles are both part of Carson's basic philosophy and a pattern for her writing. They range from the succession of the seasons to the great climatic shifts from ice age to ice age. When she uses Milton's line, "Thus with the year seasons return," to introduce "The Changing Year," she emphasizes not only the seasonal changes she will follow throughout the chapter, but the broader concept of ever-repeating yearly cycles. At the beginning of the chapter, she lists natural cycles with the effect of a litany. "For the sea as a whole, the alternation of day and night, the passage of the seasons, the procession of the years, are lost in its vastness."

For her as for other literary artists, seasonal cycles have symbolic overtones. Spring always signifies rebirth or a new beginning. "The Changing Year" begins in spring, and ends when "the fine dust of life" needs "only the touch of warming sun and fertilizing chemicals to repeat the magic of spring."

It is important to Rachel Carson that we correct our egocentric concept of the place of human beings in the natural world. "Man, in his vanity," she tells us, "subconsciously attributes a human origin to any light not of moon or stars or sun."

Carson provides the broader prospective of geologic time, so that we realize that long-term processes even now continue with a pace and scale almost beyond the comprehension of human beings who have lived on earth for only a moment of its overall history.

Although the ocean has multiple effects on our lives, Carson believes that man "cannot control or change the ocean as, in his brief tenancy of earth, he has subdued and plundered the continents." She condemns human destructiveness most strongly in "The Birth of an Island." "In a reasonable world, men would have treated these islands as precious possessions . . . valuable beyond price because nowhere in the world are they duplicated."

Carson never denies the destructiveness of nature itself—there are volcanoes, storms, and poisons—but in their scale, timing, and interrelationships, nature's hazards are part of a balanced system. Human depredations have been too massive, too frequent, and too unilateral to allow adequate compensation.

Carson does not let us lose sight of human limitations. Despite our possession of "better instruments than ever before to probe the depths of the sea, to sample its rocks and deeply layered sediments, and to read with greater clarity the dim pages of past history," there are things about the oceans and the earth we may never fully understand.

Most readers found Carson's sense of geologic time and her sweeping overviews comforting. Many wrote to tell her how reassuring it was to see the problems of their day in a broader perspective.

Although there are few quotations from eighteenth-century British writers, or references to them, in Carson's writing or notes, there is an intriguing resemblance between her ideas and those of Alexander Pope and other writers of his period. During her years as an English major, she certainly became acquainted with them. Writing *The Sea Around Us* some twenty years later, she may not have been aware of the kinship between their thought and hers.

Common to both is a belief that pattern and order govern the universe, although we are not wise enough to understand them fully. "'Tis but a Part we see, and not a whole," Pope writes.[6] Both appreciate the strength of the life force and the wonderful abundance of different forms of life. For eighteenth-century writers, this was the concept of "plenitude," according to which a great variety of beings, each differing only slightly from the next, fill the great chain of being from the lowest forms up through man and the angels to God.

In a *Spectator* essay, Joseph Addison describes the universe as swarming with a great diversity and multitude of living creatures reflecting the "exuberant and over-flowing goodness of the Supreme Being."[7] Carson's description of the development of life on volcanic islands is a remarkably close echo. "On these remote bits of earth, nature has excelled in the creation of strange and wonderful forms. As though to prove her incredible versatility, almost every island has developed species that are endemic." "Infinite goodness" has become "incredible versatility."

In the same essay, Addison anticipates the concept of ecology, commenting: "We find every mountain and marsh, wilderness and wood, plentifully stocked with birds and beasts, and every part of matter affording proper necessaries and conveniences for the livelihood of multitudes which inhabit it."

The idea of food chains, shared by Carson with other nature writers, resembles the great chain of being, although there are various interrelated groups of animals using each other for food, rather than one continuous ladder.

Like many eighteenth-century thinkers, Carson sought an explanation of the natural world that would not deny God, but did not separate the concept of deity from that of nature.

Man was no longer central to the universe in the new eighteenth-century cosmogony that showed that the sun, not the earth, was the center of the solar system. Pope writes,

> Presumptuous Man! the reason wouldst thou find,
> Why form'd so weak, so little and so blind?[8]

Carson attacks conceptual egocentricity, the belief that man is central not in a physical but in an operational and perhaps even moral sense.

When Carson describes man's "brief tenancy of earth" as "a mere moment of time," she echoes Pope's description of man's place in the universe, "His time a Moment, and a Point his space."[9]

Carson's approach to the necessity for animals to prey on and eat others is related to the attempts of earlier philosophers to rationalize the existence of evil as part of the natural order, or, for some, part of the infinity of divine goodness. Literary historian Bonamy Dobrée comments that according to eighteenth-century thought, "since they were possible, even the most horrible beasts of prey had to be, the stronger devouring the weaker."[10] Carson considers the stronger neither horrible nor evil, but whereas eighteenth-century thinkers believed that no destructive behavior was willfully evil—"whatever is, is right,"[11] Pope tells us—Carson condemns man's depredations, believing them not natural, like those of animals, but willful and controllable.

Eighteenth-century writers sought to amalgamate philosophic thinking with scientific advances, looking for rational explanations even though they considered man incapable of understanding the total scheme. Carson's approach is similar. She also believes, as they did, that literature should both please and teach.

Dobrée's summary of Pope's accomplishments in "An Essay on Man" also describes Carson's feat in *The Sea Around Us*. He transformed a compendium of information into poetry, providing a philosophic base. His work has warmth and delight and glows with wonder, although the style and language are colloquial. The structure is logical, based on intellectual not imaginative progress, but there is imaginative movement also in the tempo of the parts. Even though there are labored passages, "An Essay on Man" has sensuous appeal and is enriched by quotations which provide overtones. Above all, the author calls for intellectual humility.[12]

Today's reader of *The Sea Around Us* can choose either the original or the revised edition, published ten years later in 1961. Except for a few minor editorial changes, the texts are identical. To bring the book up to date, Carson added a preface, some items to the "Chart of the History of the Earth and Its Life" reflecting new discoveries, and an appendix containing notes linked to the text by footnote numbers and page references.

The notes contain recently discovered facts about such topics as the dating of rocks and consequent theories of the age of the earth. Carson also presents more accurate and extensive information obtained through improved instruments and undersea exploration at greater depths. Like the text of the book itself, these notes continue to remind us how much is still unknown.

The preface reviews exploration of the undersea world, concentrating on accomplishments since 1951, when the state of knowledge was "like a huge canvas on which the artist has indicated the general scheme of his grand design but on which large blank areas await the clarifying touch of his brush."

The intervening years had provided some information needed to fill in blank spaces, but had also increased Carson's concern about human depredation of our planet and the effect on oceans she had thought inviolable. Direct dumping of radioactive wastes and runoff from contaminated rivers had brought dangerous elements into the ocean, where currents were gradually distributing them worldwide. Marine creatures had been found to concentrate radiochemicals in their bodies, passing them on "up the food chain to man."

"The mistakes that are made now," Carson warns, anticipating the message she proclaims so forcefully in *Silent Spring*, "are made for all time. . . . the sea, though changed in a sinister way, will continue to exist; the threat is rather to life itself." The insights of this new preface darken the tone of the text that follows. Carson's philosophical concepts have not changed, but her preface makes the message seem more urgent.

Two new series of photographs add little to the book, since Carson's word pictures are graphic enough not to need illustration. For no apparent reason, the revised edition omits chapter numbers, a disadvantage for discussion.

Although *The Sea Around Us* is much more than a book of facts, any reader today must ask just how well its facts stand up after decades of additional research.

Nearly all the basic information about the sea is still valid, but most important, Carson provides a clear pattern so the reader can easily judge what material might be dated. We realize from her discussion that specifics like the greatest depth reached by divers, or the present status of a controversial theory or an unexplained occurrence, may no longer be accurate.

By showing us that research about the sea is a dynamic process with new facts constantly being uncovered, Carson helps us simply insert new information into the picture she has sketched out for us. After reading the book, we are even equipped to revise an area or two, if the evidence warrants.

We might read, for example, about advanced coring instruments sampling the Pacific ocean bottom two miles below the surface. They can now bring up a single core thirty-three feet long.[13] Reading Carson's discussion of information obtained from earlier, shorter cores lets us evaluate the benefits of such technological advances and integrate newly discovered facts into the total picture.

In either version, *The Sea Around Us* is a powerful synthesis of science, art, and philosophy. Nature writer Edwin Way Teale says it is "that most difficult of accomplishments, a volume that is both science *and* literature,"[14] while A. C. Spectorsky, in his anthology, *The Book of the Sea*, praises "its ability to convey the poetic quality of natural science, rather than merely popularizing its technical aspects."[15]

Even though there is some building on earlier information, each chapter can be read as an independent essay. Several appeared in magazines before book publication—"The Birth of an Island" was both the first chapter written and the first to be accepted by a major magazine[16]—and a number of chapters have been anthologized. Both philosophic import and total effect, however, come through most powerfully when the book is read as a whole.

Many nature writers emphasize the brief span of human existence set against the long stretch of evolutionary time. They are conscious also of the intimate relationship between life and the environment. Carson contributes the realization of how closely our lives are tied to events in the seas, and how powerless we are to control these events. When we act with insufficient knowledge, we too often bring about results contrary to our expectations. This is a strong argument for greater respect for the natural environment.

Carson's greatest contribution is the melding of scientific information with literary art, so that we can have a learning experience that is simultaneously an artistic delight. We leave *The Sea Around Us* able to see the oceans, and our lands within them, with keener eyes.

5

~·

Emerging from the Sea: *The Edge of the Sea*

A title-hopping trip through Rachel Carson's sea books lets us chart the evolution of her subject matter. With *Under the Sea-Wind*, Carson brings us into the drama of life in remote, mysterious places. In *The Sea Around Us*, we stay in the same vast ocean, but the more personalized title makes it seem more comfortable for the central "us."

When we reach *The Edge of the Sea*, Carson has us emerge, dripping, through the shallow waters of that region of the shore which at some point in every tidal cycle changes from sea to land. We are no longer in the breathtakingly alien world of the oceans, but the sea's edge also holds sometimes awesome surprises.

The edge of the sea, Carson tells us, constantly changes. As the tide line rises, we, like the creatures who live there, must either flee to the land or find shelter within the sea itself. This is the border zone where sea meets land, where life emerged from the sea in the course of its leisurely evolution. To Rachel Carson, this is a place of heightened significance where life is at risk, forced to adapt continually to a hostile environment. From the title onward, she makes us realize that human beings are no longer of central importance.

The territory Carson covers in *The Edge of the Sea* is narrower than in previous books. When she first began work on it, her approach was equally confined—the working title was "Guide to Seashore Life on the Atlantic

Coast"[1]—but Carson did not hesitate to radically alter her structure, no matter what the cost in rewriting, as she struggled to find the form most suitable for her content.

Her concept of the book opened up as she worked, until she found an approach that captured what she saw as the importance and implications of life at the edge of the sea. The publishers had proposed that she write a layman's guide to seashore life. Years before, she herself had described a "remote" project, "a book on the lives of shore animals."[2] Like most serious nature writers, she believed that natural history should concentrate, not on identifications or descriptions, but on the relationships of plants and animals with each other, with their surroundings, and with human beings.[3] Her problem was to reconcile the structure of a handbook with a focus on integrated lives.

As she explained to her editor, Paul Brooks, moving some facts into picture captions or "a tabular summary . . . at the end of the book" helped free her "style to be itself." The new book would be "a sort of sequel or companion volume" to *The Sea Around Us*, "the former dealing with the physical aspects of the sea, this with the biological aspects of at least part of it."[4] She never fully succeeded, however, in making this book as exciting or as breathtaking an experience as its predecessor.

Carson planted many clues to her intentions in *The Edge of the Sea*. She dedicated it to Maine friends "who have gone down with me into the low-tide world and have felt its beauty and its mystery." This reflects half of what the dust jacket advertises as the book's "double purpose." Facts and pictures make it a helpful guide, but Carson wants to stimulate not only investigation, but aesthetic and emotional responses as well.

Her unstated third purpose is to influence our basic attitudes, strengthening, or, if necessary, creating a sense of the sanctity of all forms of life, and of the earth itself.

Even as a guidebook, *The Edge of the Sea* is unusual. Carson points out in the preface that the three coastal areas whose descriptions form the central portion of the book—rocky shore, sand beach, and coral reef—are typical of basic shore types of the world, so that the book transcends its specific subject. In addition, Carson provides no answers to specific questions, or prescriptions of what to look at, only a companion who discourses knowledgeably about what we may find and what it all means.

Her brief opening chapter, "The Marginal World," is a series of "recollections of places that have stirred me deeply." She introduces two basic concepts: the interrelationship of all forms of life; and geologic time, in which history begins with the formation of the earth. Carson emphasizes the importance of understanding shoreline life to full knowledge of our world.

The second chapter, "Patterns of Shore Life," explains the effects on shore animals and vegetation of surf, currents, and tides. Influencing the effects of these forces, we learn, are the nature of the coast, the action of the water, and the strength of the tides. The contents of the water play their role, determining the availability of food and chemical substances. All these factors interrelate to build the "intricate design of the fabric of life."

Carson opens chapter 3, "The Rocky Shores," with geologic background, then describes, one by one, the sea creatures and plants that live among the rocks. She gives us life histories, reproductive details, and any other information relevant to understanding of their lives.

The seaweed kelp provides a transition to another group of creatures, who find shelter among the kelp's holdfasts, rootlike structures which grasp the rocks. The chapter ends with an extended look at life in a particularly beautiful tide pool hidden in a cave among the rocks.

Carson moves south along the Atlantic coast for her fourth chapter, "The Rim of Sand." After explaining

how each grain of sand is the result of long geological
processes, she describes the forms of life within the sand,
"the abundant life of protected beaches and shoals, the
sparse life of surf-swept sands, and the pioneering life
that has reached the high-tide line and seems poised in
space and time for invasion of the land."

Then she examines the flotsam on the beach, records
of "other lives," including the dangerous Portuguese
man-of-war. She shows us how to interpret the subtle
hints, in these bits of sponge and shells and "bones of
fishes" and "feathers of birds," of a tropical climate
nearby, or "the intrusion of cold water from the north."
Explaining the signs of lives elsewhere, Carson adds
lively details about the far-off creatures whose remains
have reached this shore. The ramshorn shell, "a small
white spiral forming two or three loose coils," is the only
part to reach shore of the squidlike Spirula, a deep-sea
animal with ten arms and a cylindrical body with pro-
pellerlike fins, which swims with "jerky, backward
spurts of jet-propelled motion."

Moving south again to "The Coral Coast" of Florida,
in chapter 5, Carson quickly establishes its unusual atmosphere—a sense of the past in its coral composition,
of the present in its tropical growths, and of the future
in its still expanding coral reefs and mangrove swamps.

With her skillful combination of broad sweep and
pertinent detail, she sketches in all the background we
need from geology, geography, and history. Again the
primary focus is lives—the coral animal itself and other
reef creatures like the palolo, which swarms in the moonlight.

From the turtle grass of the reef flats, with its pipefish and sea horses, Carson moves to the mangrove
forests whose arching roots continually extend their islands into the sea, trapping debris which becomes new
soil to support new mangrove trees. This chapter ends
as Florida does, with the sea that bathes the edges of the

mangrove swamps, the sea whose actions will determine the future of these shores.

This transition carries Carson directly into her concluding chapter, "The Enduring Sea," where she returns to personal experience. Hearing the tide rising on her own stretch of rocky coast in Maine, she remembers all the coastal areas, united by the sea and subject to its transforming powers.

The "Appendix: Classification" follows traditional scientific order. Carson describes simple one-celled animals and plants like the *Dinoflagellata*, an indeterminate group claimed by both zoologists and botanists, then proceeds through the more complex chordates, "forerunners of the vertebrates, or backboned animals."

Rather than skim over whole classifications, she limits herself to selected examples, choosing the ascidians or sea squirts, for example, as "the most common representatives on the shore of that interesting group of early chordates, the Tunicata." She combines life histories and biological details with facts from history, literature, and commerce. We learn how the sea squirt earned its name—by forcing jets of water through its tubular openings—and that brown seaweeds were once used in the production of iodine.

Throughout *The Edge of the Sea*, Carson presents facts clearly and thoroughly, yet with grace enough to prevent the book from becoming a text or traditional handbook. On the first page, the shore is defined by implication, rather than statement, as the area between the tide lines, an example of her subtle exposition.

Topics like the relationship of life cycles to tides and moon are developed with examples ranging from ancient legend to current research, while comparison of three kinds of periwinkles provides a living demonstration of how animals evolve from marine to land forms.

Difficult concepts become remarkably clear. Explaining how small beaches form on predominantly rocky coasts, she concludes: "These occasional sandy or pebbly beaches are almost always in protected, incurving shores or dead-end coves, where the waves can deposit debris but from which they cannot easily remove it."

Sometimes the teaching is less subtle. "The conjunction of strong tides and a rocky shore, where much of the life is exposed," she announces, "creates . . . a beautiful demonstration of the power of the tides over living things." The intricate relationships of shoreline creatures, however, are demonstrated without comment when she shows how limpets, by scraping rocks clean, "render a service to barnacles," whose larvae can then more easily attach themselves. "Indeed," she concludes, with an image characteristic of her best work, "the paths radiating out from a limpet's home are sometimes marked by a sprinkling of the starlike shells of young barnacles."

Carson guides the reader's own explorations without specific instructions. She comments that the "black zone," made up of minute plants found just above "the area that clearly belongs to the sea," is slippery, subtly implying the need for caution, and mentions her own need for a hand lens to look at infant snails.

Much of the documentation for *The Edge of the Sea* came from Carson's own research and observations, but she sought help when she needed it. An expert identified specimens from Myrtle Beach as "worm rock," the first known examples from the Atlantic coast. As an active marine biologist, she also personalizes scientific material to make it more accessible. Her discovery of "a curious little mollusk . . . among Florida's Ten Thousand Islands" illustrates the transport and dispersal of marine animals.

We know from Carson's letters and papers that she did extensive reading, as well as field research, to prepare for *The Edge of the Sea*, but neither the acknowledgments nor the text show the abundance of consultations and references to authorities found in *The Sea Around Us*.

Despite the lack of explicit documentation, however, Carson always weighs her statements of fact. "Ghost crabs and beach fleas are believed to dig very deep holes . . . and go into hibernation" contrasts with the straightforward "Mole crabs . . . retire to the bottom offshore in winter."

Carson did not always agree with traditional scientific attitudes. "For the convenience of those who like to pigeonhole their findings neatly in the classification schemes the human mind has devised," she writes in her preface, "an appendix presents the conventional groups, or phyla."

Carson enlivens her writing by dipping into etymology, history, mythology, and literature. We learn that spring tides got their names not from the season but from the Saxon *springen*, meaning strong active movement, while the expression *neap* comes from the old Scandinavian for barely touching. The information is both a diversion and a teaching device.

Seeing the sea hare of the Florida Keys, she tells us that the Roman writer "Pliny declared it was poisonous to the touch, and recommended as an antidote asses' milk and ground asses' bones, boiled together." A century later, she adds, Apuleius, who wrote *The Golden Ass*, was accused of witchcraft when he persuaded two fishermen to bring him a sea hare to examine. Further examination had to wait fifteen centuries, until 1684. This historical sidelight tells us as much about forces that affect scientific research as about sea hares.

Carson borrows a touch of humor from *Alice in Wonderland* when she pictures a rockweed forest as "a fantastic jungle, mad in a Lewis Carroll sort of way. For what proper jungle, twice every twenty-four hours, begins to sag lower and lower and finally lies prostrate for several hours, only to rise again?"

She continually varies her rhetorical techniques. The sense-oriented description, "The grains of dry sands rub one against another," not only expands our sensitivity to sound and tactile sensations, but makes us share the physical perspective of animals burrowing there.

Interlocking paragraphs reflect environmental relationships. A description of periwinkles so persistently scraping rocks that they must constantly bring forward new teeth is followed by a discussion of the effects of the scraping on the rocks themselves.

Well aware of the power of specific detail, Carson moves from a general statement about the ever-present coastal "black zone" to examples of these minute plants on "the smooth platform of coquina at St. Augustine" and "the concrete jetties at Beaufort."

She introduces the excitement of following events as they happen when she describes recent scientific discoveries about the responses of plants to the phases of the moon. "It appears," she tells us, "that we may be on the verge of solving some of the riddles that have plagued men's minds for centuries."

Her precise choice of words combines scientific exactness with a poetic complexity of meanings. In the chapter title, "The Marginal World," *margin* not only means "edge," but also suggests the marginal or precarious existence of both living things and the shoreline itself, always shifting and changing in response to the forces of the sea.

Carson's writing shows consciousness of pattern and unity at every level. The overall pattern has two primary elements, rhetorical movement from recollection to exposition, and geographical movement southward along the Atlantic coast of the United States, from rocky coast, through sandy beaches, to the coral coast of Florida.

These movements are repeated on a smaller scale throughout the book. In the chapter of recollections, for example, Carson remembers experiences first on the rocky shores of Maine, then on sandy beaches, and finally on the coral coast. She chooses experiences that create a sense of the shore as an alien, primeval world, removed from the ordinary realities of the land. Periodic renewal of this atmosphere creates a unifying mood.

The pattern of rising and falling tides governs the shore chapters, followed with particular faithfulness in "The Rocky Shores," where she moves, each time more slowly, through a series of tidal cycles.

The discussion of sea hares illustrates the pattern of her life histories, although the particular elements included differ in each case. First, her own experience: the sudden appearance of a group of tropical sea hares off Ohio Key in Florida. Recollection of another experience in the Carolinas lets her compare the two varieties of sea hares.

Physical description and classification follow, accompanied by a historical narrative ranging back to Roman times. After a brief life history, Carson introduces a broader perspective, relating the sea hares' lives to long-term processes such as the echinoderms' place in the economy of the sea world, with its constant recirculation of materials. Moving to yet larger circles of meaning, she concludes with "geologic processes of earth building and earth destruction," in which sea-hare skeletons contribute calcium to the building of a reef.

Nonscientists new to marine life may be disturbed by occasional lapses in exposition—*chitinous*, for example, used without explanation to describe the shell of the lobster—but all readers will appreciate Carson's lack of condescension and her accurate scientific terminology.

In Carson's earlier books, patterns of sexual activity or childcare different from the ordinary were consistently presented without comment. In this book, usage varies. She simply states that the sea hare may function as either sex or both, but tells us that the pipefish "begins life in a strange manner, being developed, nurtured, and reared beyond the stage of helpless infancy by the male parent, who keeps his young within a protective pouch."

The same information sometimes appears more than once, such as the explanation of how free passage between the Atlantic and Pacific oceans was blocked by a ridge of land which arose between the American continents. This is mentioned in various explanations of species migration and differentiation.

Describing "the extraordinary course" of development of the sea pansy, where a single minute larva becomes a colony of many individuals, Carson ignores the fact that she has already shown the same course of development in other animals.

Early in the coral coast chapter, however, she makes appropriate comparisons, showing how the vermetid snail of the coral reefs, the New England barnacle, and the mole crab of the southern beaches each adapt to a sedentary existence.

Carson's hallmark, as always, is the combination of scientific precision with literary artistry, but the level of artistry is less consistent in *The Edge of the Sea*. When she plunges into exploration of "The Rocky Shores" after two chapters of unexciting background material, there is a surge of vitality, with sentences and passages soaring to accumulated intensity through patterns of sound, rhythm, and grammatical structure, while descriptions of rising and falling tides gracefully imitate the movements of the water.

She describes the unrest of rising water, "with the surge leaping high over jutting rocks and running in lacy cascades of foam over the landward side of massive boulders," and the more peaceful ebb, when "rocks that the high tide had concealed rise into view and glisten with the wetness left on them by the receding water."

The density of alliteration and assonance increases with the concreteness of the writing. Besides obvious examples like "sparkling at the surface of the sea," we find subtler sound combinations. In "the shells of mollusks, the spines of sea urchins, the opercula of snails," repeated *s*'s and *l*'s interact with the movement between open and closed vowels.

"I hope some of the fascination I feel has seeped through into the book," Carson told a Houghton Mifflin sales conference.[5] Without diminishing the usefulness of tide pools as scientific examples, she turns them into fascinating verbal equivalents of paintings with multiple levels of artistic illusion.

They are "mysterious worlds . . . where all the beauty of the sea is subtly suggested and portrayed in miniature." One pool

transcends its realities of rock and water and plants, and out of these elements creates the illusion of . . . [a] world . . . of hills and valleys with scattered forests. Yet the illusion is not so much that of an actual landscape as of a painting of one; . . . the artistry of the pool, as of the painter, creates the image and the impression.

The pools are thus beautiful in themselves, as natural phenomena; beautiful pictures of landscapes; and, at the same time, artistic miniatures of the sea. Through illusion, Carson both mimics and transforms reality, simultaneously demonstrating her philosophy of interconnection by linking the sea and the land.

To create all her word pictures, Carson makes liberal use of color, sense impressions, and imagery. Delicate hues dominate her first impression of the rocky coast's intertidal zone: greens, whites, and browns ranging to cream; then tide pools which are "gardens of color"— green and ocher-yellow, pale pink, bronze, electric-blue, and old-rose.

She evokes our sense of touch, as well as the more common sight and hearing. As she peers into a "fairy cave," we feel the "wet carpet of sea moss" she kneels on, while sight and sound combine as "water trickles and gurgles and cascades in miniature waterfalls."

Sea smells add an extra layer of impression, their pervasiveness reinforced by word repetition.

And over it all there is the smell of low tide, compounded of the faint, pervasive smell of worms and snails and jellyfish and crabs—the sulphur smell of sponge, the iodine smell of rockweed, and the salt smell of the rime that glitters on the sundried rocks.

Similes and metaphors create pleasing effects while providing familiar comparisons for exotic subjects. Among the tentacles of the tube worm, *Spirorbis*, is its operculum, or covering plate, "a structure like a long-stemmed goblet," while "in the inmost coils of the tube" are developing eggs, like "little chains of beads wrapped in cellophane." These references to decorative art reinforce her concept of natural art.

Strangeness, like beauty, is suggested through imagery: a green weed is "stringy as mermaids' hair," while sanderlings scurry "like little ghosts." In her accurate yet fantastic bestiary, stone crabs live "in dark little dens of the sea floor." "About their lairs, as about the abodes of legendary giants, lie the broken remains of their prey."

In an image that explodes into full-blown fantasy, mole crabs come to the surface of the sand to feed "as though a host of strange little troglodytes had momentarily looked out through the curtains of their hidden world and as abruptly retired within it."

Figures of speech also make the sea world seem pragmatically ordered and commonplace. As in an industrial process, rocks are "splintered by the chisels of the frost, crushed under advancing glaciers . . . then ground and polished in the mill of the surf."

To picture the small anemones living in empty holes in beach timbers, Carson has us visualize "in each hole . . . a dark glistening body like a raisin embedded in a cake," while the pipe fish sucks in tiny crustaceans "through the tube-like beak, as one would suck a soda through a straw."

Carson frequently draws comparisons from the land

world to make this alien world familiar and further reinforce her sense of "the ancient unity" between land and
sea. The rose tellin, a mollusk, looks like "scattered petals
of pink roses," while the infant barnacle's radical change
into adult form is like the metamorphosis of the larval
butterfly.

Images are usually fresh and dramatic, like islands
"putting boldly out to sea," but there are traces of tired
language in expressions like "crystal clear." Long
stretches of competent but undistinguished writing keep
this book from equaling *The Sea Around Us*. They are
often redeemed, however, with a sudden striking image
like this metaphor, which captures the essence of a whole
group of animals: "Many of the hydroids, so like flow-
ering plants in appearance, shrink down to the very core
of their animal beings in winter, withdrawing all living
tissues into the basal stalk."

Carson always writes with controlled rhythm but
some passages take on the patterns of poetry. The
rhythms of the title, which is also the opening phrase of
the book, dominate the opening pages—the edge of the
sea (' / ' ' /).

Some passages can be read as lines of poetry:

  '   / ' ' '   / '   /
And so in that enchanted place

' '   / / ' ' /
on the threshold of the sea

  ' '/ ' / '   ' /   ' /
the realities that possessed my mind

  '   / '   / '   ' /   /
were far from those of the land world

' ' / '   /   ' /
I had left an hour before.

Although its overall effect is didactic, *The Edge of the
Sea* most closely resembles a personal essay in the manner

of Thoreau and other predecessors in natural history, with passages of exposition or description within an over-all tone of intimacy. It takes us on a journey down and up the Atlantic coast, but unlike most books of natural history based on journeys, it is neither geographically consecutive nor chronological. Carson moves by thematic associations—one visit to a cave, for example, reminds her of another.

Like other nature writers, she uses small units of experience to shape units of reporting. In her visit to a sea cave at the end of "The Rocky Shores," she blends the visit with others to the same pool, then takes us fur-ther backward in time through a brief history of the ever-present sponges. She closes with a broad view of this "present that is but a moment," concretely realized by the simultaneous presence of ancient sponges, a fish whose ancestry is "traceable only half as far into the past," and herself, "in whose eyes . . . the two were . . . contemporaries, . . . a mere newcomer whose ancestors had inhabited the earth so briefly that my presence was almost anachronistic."

Carson's basic philosophy in *The Edge of the Sea* is ecological. The preface sets the tone.

To understand the life of the shore, it is not enough to pick up an empty shell and say "This is a murex," or "That is an angel wing." True understanding demands intuitive comprehension of the whole life of the creature that once inhabited this empty shell: how it survived amid surf and storms, what were its ene-mies, how it found food and reproduced its kind, what were its relations to the particular sea world in which it lived.

"I have tried," she concludes, "to interpret the shore in terms of that essential unity that binds life to the earth."

Chapter summaries are explicitly philosophic. As she closes "Patterns of Shore Life," she comments, "For it is now clear that in the sea nothing lives to itself. . . .

So the present is linked with past and future, and each living thing with all that surrounds it."

General statements are grounded in supporting detail. "Barring catastrophe," Carson writes, "the forces that destroy neither outweigh nor are outweighed by those that create, and over the years of a man's life, as over the ages of recent geologic time, the total number of mussels on the shore probably has remained about the same."

Even Carson is sometimes appalled by the huge numbers of creatures that do not survive. Seeing anemones in beach timbers, "one is struck anew by the enormous waste of life, remembering that for each of these anemones that succeeded in finding a home, many thousands must have failed."

This contrasts with Carson's usual interpretation of such circumstances as a demonstration of the strength of the life force. On the following page, she describes "that ceaseless migration, for the most part doomed to futility, yet ensuring that always, when opportunity arises, Life shall be waiting, ready to take advantage."

This biologic imperative becomes a dominant theme. In "The Rocky Shores," "blindly searching larvae . . . drift in the ocean currents ready to colonize . . . or to die." In "The Rim of Sand," "failure turns into success when, for all the billions lost, a few succeed."

Carson is conscious of various balances in nature, including the relationship between risk and security. Describing the lives of creatures who bore into rock, piers, or timbers to escape the surf, she comments: "All of these creatures have exchanged their freedom for a sanctuary from the waves, being imprisoned forever within the chambers they have carved."

The Edge of the Sea is more limited than Carson's two previous sea books. Parts of the world beyond the eastern shore of the United States appear only in occasional examples or comparisons. Some deep-sea creatures are mentioned when their shells or other remains are found on the beach, but Carson generally confines herself to life within the tidelines.

Even appreciative reviewers noted the difference. Jonathan Leonard wrote in the *New York Times* that Carson was not dealing "with the sea as a majestic whole." He missed "the organ tones" of *The Sea Around Us*.[6]

Other reviewers missed an amplitude they labeled "cosmic." Fanny Butcher in the *Chicago Sunday Tribune* thought readers "awaiting eagerly" Carson's new book "will be rewarded, but not in the same terms of world and cosmic implications,"[7] while Robert Cushman Murphy in the *New York Herald Tribune Book Review* foresaw that the book might "prove less compelling than her Odyssean account of cosmic forces at work in the sea."[8]

Most reviewers praised Carson's artistry, described somewhat extravagantly by *Time* magazine as "her remarkable talent for catching the life breath of science on the still glass of poetry."[9]

Although *The Edge of the Sea*, like *The Sea Around Us*, was a best-seller, few read it or remember it today. Shore areas are more accessible than the deep sea, but less exciting. A dramatic style draws more readers than relaxed intimacy.

Form remains a problem. Even the relegation of many details to the appendix does not eliminate an occasional feeling of wading through a catalog of sea creatures.

The book is also flawed by repetitions and heavy reliance on emotional reactions. Glorifying the young starfish's "clean perfection of form and structure," she writes: "There is an obvious newness about them, proclaiming that they have undergone their metamorphosis from the larval form to the adult shape only recently." The image is pleasant, but unlike most of Carson's work, this is a judgment without supporting specifics. The observation would be difficult to apply in our own explorations.

Carson was working at a lower level in *The Edge of the Sea*, a book written during the first hectic stages of her unexpected fame. But Carson's lower level is still writing of a higher quality than most guidebooks to the shore or nature books about the sea. Her cogent philosophy and exuberant enthusiasm are a special bonus.

The book also has some quietly dazzling high points. Describing the flowerlike hydroid *Tubularia* in the opening chapter, Carson unobtrusively mingles exposition of a general idea with specific facts and her basic philosophy. *Tubularia* is a creature of fragile beauty whose every part is functionally useful and adroitly fashioned to take advantage of the environment. The description demonstrates ecological relationships, nature's economy, and the strength of the life force, yet also gives us a specific example we will be able to recognize.

Carson leaves us with a combined sense of constant change and the need to learn more. Once sand, the rocky coast will one day be sand again. "As the shore configuration changes in the flow of time, the pattern of life changes, never static, never quite the same from year to year."

6

A Book for our Time: *Silent Spring*

Whether great men create history or are themselves created by their times is a question that has never been resolved. The probable answer is that circumstances draw forth latent talents so that greatness flares.

In 1962 there was an author of great talent and scientific acuity, a subject—chemical pollution of the environment—about to explode, and a receptive audience prepared by disturbing hints and specific alarms.

Just before Thanksgiving in 1959, cranberries contaminated with the weed killer aminotriazole, known to cause cancer in rats at even low doses, had had to be withdrawn from the market. Then followed the thalidomide tragedies, when mothers who had taken the drug during pregnancy gave birth to severely deformed children.

Carson recognized the impact of these incidents on the public. "By what may be the fortunate chance that I am a slow writer . . . *Silent Spring* was published about two years later than my original plans called for." An isolated problem had become part of the "sorry whole—the reckless pollution of our living world with harmful and dangerous substances."[1] Just at the right moment, all the elements—writer, subject, audience—came together in synergy to produce a masterpiece.

Two later books, *Before Silent Spring* and *Since Silent Spring*[2] are testimony to *Silent Spring*'s effect. James

Whorton, in *Before Silent Spring*, believes Carson's book began a new kind of writing about pesticides while it brought "the previously simmering discontent with DDT to a boil and made insecticidal contamination of food and the environment a subject of national alarm."[3]

The chairman of the Book-of-the-Month Club's board of directors warned members not to reject this book that was "certain to be history-making in its influence upon thought and public policy over the world."[4]

Yet Carson had never intended to undertake a project as all-consuming as *Silent Spring* became. She had planned to write a book not about pesticides, but on the broadly philosophical topic of human beings and the natural world.

Two events led her back to DDT, which she had proposed as a subject to the *Reader's Digest* in 1945.[5] A friend, concerned about terrible bird deaths after aerial spraying with DDT, asked Carson to seek help in Washington to combat future mass spraying. She also learned of a Long Island court case in which residents sought to prevent their property from being sprayed with DDT as part of a gypsy moth control program.

Preliminary research made her realize the magnitude and seriousness of the pesticide problem. "The facts had to be brought together in one place," she told the Women's National Book Association in 1963. "I could not rest until I had brought them to public attention."[6]

At first she planned only a magazine article that would also serve as a chapter of a book she could introduce and edit, but as one lead led to another, both material and future work multiplied. When *The New Yorker* asked for twenty or thirty thousand words, she thought this would be the basis of a "short book," to be published in 1959.[7]

In 1959, however, she wrote to her editor, Paul Brooks, that "in the end I believe you will feel, as I do, that my long and thorough preparation is indispensable to doing an effective job. . . . Now it is as though all the pieces of an extremely complex jigsaw puzzle are at last falling into place."

She explained her intentions for the book: "principal emphasis to the menace to human health, even though setting this within the general framework of disturbances of the basic ecology of all living things"; "a synthesis of widely scattered facts" building "a really damning case against the use of these chemicals as they are now inflicted upon us"; particular concern "with the slow, cumulative and hard-to-identify long-term effects." She would also emphasize the positive approach, such as biological controls, as alternatives to chemical sprays.[8]

To her colleague Shirley Briggs, the tremendously positive public response to *Silent Spring* was a reflection of Carson's attitude toward life and "the quality of her feeling for nature." "Her subject in this, her last book was the misuse of our environment with chemical contaminants but her goal was, as always, to bring her fellow men to understand something of the whole wondrous complex of life."[9] This emphasis on life is particularly remarkable in a book written under the tremendous pressures of multiple illnesses and growing awareness of her approaching death.

Neither title nor dedication, however, are positive in tone. Editor Paul Brooks suggested "Silent Spring," at first for the bird chapter alone. Later, when they could find nothing else more appealing than "Man Against the Earth," he convinced Carson that with the motto from Keats,

> The sedge is wither'd from the lake,
> And no birds sing.

supplied by Carson's literary agent, Marie Rodell, "the image of 'silent spring' symbolized the theme of the book as a whole."[10]

The dedication—"To Albert Schweitzer who said

'Man has lost the capacity to foresee and to forestall. He will end by destroying the earth'"—is more pessimistic than another Schweitzer phrase Carson often quoted, "reverence for life."

Carson sets the scene with "A Fable for Tomorrow," a stark composite picture of a town devastated by pesticides. Everything in this account has happened, Carson assures us, but not all in one place.

After this highly dramatic prologue comes "The Obligation to Endure," an introductory declaration of humanity's destructive interaction with the environment. Within the perspective of the long history of the earth, our period of technological capability to change our environment has been brief, but we are already adding to the known dangers of radiation similar but unrecognized dangers posed by chemicals. Because ignorance may bring disaster, Carson emphasizes our obligation to gain knowledge and shape our actions accordingly, so that we may endure.

This nodding acquaintance with the dangers of chemicals prepares us for the third chapter, where Carson thoroughly introduces us to the history, descriptions, and effects of known pesticides and herbicides, in order of their advancing strength and poisonousness.

With the sinister characters in place, the action begins in chapter 4, the first of eleven chapters analyzing the effects of pesticides and herbicides on the natural world and life within it. Carson first demonstrates the pollution of our water system and soil, then damage to plants and wildlife, and finally the more obvious kills of birds and fish. The ninth chapter emphasizes a point that reverberates throughout the book, the scarcity of money for research into the effects of pesticides, or for the search for other methods of control.

Using government campaigns to control the gypsy moth and the fire ant as examples, Carson displays the disastrous results of aerial spraying in chapter 10. In the next chapter she moves from the immediate effects of massive doses of pesticides to the insidious action of constant exposure to small doses. Continuous accumulation of various man-made chemicals in our bodies, she suggests, may ultimately pose the greatest danger.

The three following chapters deal specifically with that issue. "The Human Price" describes new environmental health problems resulting from radiation and chemicals, their ultimate outcome unknown. After summarizing effects on soil, water, food, fish, and birds, she tells us that "Man, however much he may like to pretend the contrary, is part of nature. Can he escape a pollution that is now so thoroughly distributed throughout our world?" For us "as for the robin in Michigan or the salmon in the Miramichi, this is a problem of ecology, of interrelationships, of interdependence."

Chapter 12 concludes with a detailed discussion of the effects of pesticides on the liver and the nervous system, while chapter 13 focuses on pesticide-induced changes within the cell that affect the basic processes of life.

Next Carson attacks what became the most controversial topic in *Silent Spring*, chemical exposure and cancer. With detailed scientific evidence, she links cancer and radiation, and cancer and both natural and man-made substances, including pesticides. Then she presents the latest theories on the origin of cancer in the cell.

The three concluding chapters balance the three opening chapters. First Carson shows how nonselective spraying upsets the balance of nature. Natural controls, she maintains, are a positive alternative. Then she demonstrates the failures and inefficiencies of pesticides, concentrating particularly on development of resistant species. We too might ultimately develop resistance, but human generations come so slowly that it would take hundreds or thousands of years.

Carson closes the book by urging us to give up our

misguided fight against nature. We must work with natural processes instead, by developing better methods of biological control. No less than the destruction or preservation of the earth is our choice.

Silent Spring takes the form of densely packed argument, moving from the exhortation to endure to cogent specific suggestions. Interrelated ideas, central to one topic, peripheral to others, and common examples, such as the fire ant or Japanese beetle programs, brought formidable organizational problems, so that occasional repetition and cross references are unavoidable.

Logical development and recurrent themes, motifs, and images provide overall unity and structural interrelationships. The opening "Fable," for example, introduces the killing of birds, wildflowers, and fish. These deaths become symptoms and ultimately symbols of the inadvertent side effects of pesticide use.

The phrase "present road," used in the second chapter to describe our current actions, foreshadows the final chapter, "The Other Road," which presents other options. Neighboring chapters are similarly connected. At the beginning of her chapter on the soil, Carson uses the phrase "the earth's green mantle," the title of the following chapter. That chapter opens: "Water, soil, and the earth's green mantle of plants make up the world that supports the animal life of the earth."

Titles are echoed either at the beginning or end of chapters. Chapter 2 ends, "In the words of Jean Rostand, 'The obligation to endure gives us the right to know.'"

The last sentence in chapter 11, "As matters stand now, we are in little better position than the guests of the Borgias," refers not only to the title, "Beyond the Dreams of the Borgias," but also to the thematic use of the Borgias as prototypical poisoners. Carson describes arsenic earlier in the book as an agent of homicide "from long before the time of the Borgias."

Her ability to present complex scientific material

with beauty as well as clarity greatly contributes to the effectiveness of *Silent Spring*. Although a superb picture of the formation of soil and the interaction of creatures within it is reminiscent of passages on the minute denizens of the sea in earlier books, the expository demands imposed on the author in *Silent Spring* are far greater.

Carson must explain complex material such as the chemical structure of chlorinated hydrocarbons and organic phosphorus compounds, the two large groups of modern insecticides, to the nonscientist. All of these compounds are built on the basis of carbon atoms, the building blocks of the living world, which explains how they can interfere with the processes of life.

She establishes the unknown as carefully as the proven, noting that "the chemists' ingenuity in devising insecticides has long ago outrun biological knowledge of the way these poisons affect the living organism."

The discussion of attempts to save forest trees through massive spraying, in "And No Birds Sing," demonstrates her thorough presentation of information. First, the cycle of destruction—"the poison was spreading through the food chain, reaching out from the seed eaters to the furred and feathered carnivores." Then side effects from the loss of natural controls—woodpeckers, for example, eat destructive spruce beetles and codling moths. Next a presentation of the results of nonchemical means, such as sanitary disposal of diseased materials practiced in New York.

Introducing a broader approach, Carson explains the importance of "the conservation of variety," in British ecologist Charles Elton's words. Large areas planted with single species allow the easy spread of disease. Finally she shows how bird populations are further decimated—eagles are a prime example—when genetic damage prevents live births.

Her method is to integrate technical explanations, broad discussion, narrative examples, and personal accounts from her own experience and those of others. She even slips in practical advice: insecticide residues on food "are little affected by washing—the only remedy is to remove and discard all outside leaves of such vegetables as lettuce or cabbage, to peel fruit and to use no skins or outer covering whatever. Cooking does not destroy residues."

Summaries enforce our learning process. She writes of "health problems . . . born of the never-ending stream of chemicals of which pesticides are a part, chemicals now pervading the world in which we live, acting upon us directly and indirectly, separately and collectively."

Anticipating controversy, Carson provided fifty-five pages of notes documenting her sources, references throughout the text to specific authorities, and a lengthy list of acknowledgments, including sixteen experts who had read and commented on portions of the manuscript.

Her collected papers further demonstrate her exhaustive research. There are file drawers of scientific reprints, conference reports, congressional testimony, newspaper articles, and letters ranging from expert testimony in answer to her technical questions to personal accounts of illness or observations.[11]

Scientists have learned a great deal about chemicals and diseases since 1962. In the cancer field, experts tell us that "Our knowledge of the factors involved in the development of human cancers, although incomplete, has increased greatly over the past few decades and, especially, in the past two decades"[12]—precisely the period since *Silent Spring* was written.

Nonetheless, the scientific reliability of *Silent Spring* today is remarkable. As in *The Sea Around Us*, the general framework and propositions remain valid, even when specifics or interpretations have been modified. New evidence fits right in.

Carson was able to pinpoint the most important findings and capture their essence in a few clear sentences.

She discusses two theories of the origin of cancer cells: the genetic theory that cancer results from chromosome damage; and German scientist Otto Warburg's theory that the cell's normal method of energy production, respiration, is destroyed and replaced by an abnormal method, fermentation, which is passed on to descendant cells.

Warburg's theory is little discussed in recent scientific reports, but is by no means discredited. Newly developed sophisticated techniques to measure energy within the cell now make it possible to investigate its validity.[13]

Recent scientific literature generally focuses on the genetic theory, expressed now in terms of changes in DNA, the chemical carrier of the genetic message within the chromosome. Despite significant gains in knowledge in the years since *Silent Spring*, Carson's description of the genetic theory is still generally valid.

According to the mutation theory of the origin of cancer, a cell, perhaps under the influence of radiation or of a chemical, develops a mutation that allows it to escape the controls the body normally asserts over cell division. It is therefore able to multiply in a wild and unregulated manner. The new cells resulting from these divisions have the same ability to escape control.

Drs. Elizabeth and James Miller, in a special supplement to *Cancer*, write:

Of the known carcinogenic agents (viruses, ultraviolet and ionizing radiations, and chemicals), chemicals appear to be of major importance in the induction of human cancers. . . . The available data indicate that initiation generally results from one or more mutations of cellular DNA. The second stage, promotion, takes a longer period of time. Sometimes different chemicals initiate and promote. "Complete carcinogens" do both.[14]

Carson was aware of the concepts of initiation and promotion, and of the interaction of chemicals to compound the damage (potentiation). Summarizing a discussion of herbicides and skin tumors, she writes:

Cancer may sometimes require the complementary action of two chemicals, one of which sensitizes the cell or tissue so that it may later, under the action of another or promoting agent, develop true malignancy. Thus, the herbicides IPC and CIPC may act as initiators in the production of skin tumors, sowing the seeds of malignancy that may be brought into actual being by something else—perhaps a common detergent.

All too many areas in which Carson identifies our need for knowledge remain inconclusively studied today. After discussing the effects of DDT on the liver, Carson concludes, "No one yet knows what the ultimate consequences may be." In his recent authoritative text on damage to the liver, Dr. Hyman Zimmerman repeatedly comments on "grossly insufficient" data and "woefully inadequate" studies, urging that there be further investigation.[15]

When Zimmerman introduces the subject of potential liver damage from environmental pollution, he credits Carson with opening "the era of concerned focus on the problem." Even though he qualifies his conclusions because of the lack of data, many of his statements are remarkably similar to hers.

Carson strongly believed that DDT would be proven harmful to human beings, but this has not yet been borne out by research. Zimmerman cites proven liver damage in animals, but in humans, he states that "Despite the billions of pounds of DDT that have been manufactured and used, no instance of hepatic injury acquired as the result of occupational or environmental exposure has yet been attributed to it."

He concludes, however: "Reassuring as is the lack of overt hepatic injury from DDT on ordinary exposure . . . the resolution of the long-term threat of this agent to the liver is more complicated. . . . The essential epidemiologic studies . . . remain to be performed." Zimmerman substantiates Carson's indictments of other organic pesticides such as Aldrin and Dieldrin as proven dangerous.

The most important potentially adverse effect of DDT and other contaminating chemicals, according to Zimmerman, may be their alteration of the function of enzyme systems, changing responses to other agents, and perhaps strengthening the potential of other chemicals to damage the liver or cause cancer.

"Indeed," he writes, "the devastating effects in the ecosystem that appear to have been wrought by DDT are ascribable to the induction of the drug-metabolizing enzyme systems. Altered metabolism of sex hormones by birds, for example, has led to the laying of nonviable eggs and to the near eradiction of some species."

Carson urges that public officials responsible for the decisions on pesticide use be acquainted with scientific evidence about risks. Discussing sterility in animals caused by the chemical Aldrin, she declares, "No one knows whether the same effect will be seen in human beings, yet this chemical has been sprayed from airplanes over suburban areas and farmlands."

In a recent review of causes of cancer, Dr. David Schottenfeld notes the lack of "any simplistic interpretation of causation," but concludes that "there appears to be general agreement that most cancers are associated to some degree with environmental factors." His recommendations are much like Carson's. "The implementation of preventive measures, the transfer of scientific technology to the decision-making process of regulatory agencies, and the modification of human behavior are the ultimate challenges of preventive oncology." [16]

Carson wrote not only for fellow scientists but for the general public. Nonetheless the contrast between her style and that of most scientific writing, like the example above, helps explain her distinctive power to influence readers.

She begins each chapter with a purposeful statement that she elaborates, moving from general statements to support statements to specific details. "Elixirs of Death" begins: "For the first time in the history of the world, every human being is now subjected to contact with dangerous chemicals, from the moment of conception until death." This topic sentence tells us she will cover historical development of chemicals, their nature and dangerous effects, and their ubiquitous presence.

A general statement about "simpler inorganic insecticides of prewar days" is followed by general examples such as "compounds of arsenic, copper," and then particular examples like "pyrethrum from the dried flowers of chrysanthemums." Carson draws details from common experience, asking, for example, whether the threat of genetic damage is "not too high a price to pay for a sproutless potato or a mosquitoless patio?"

Carson uses the connotations of words, as well as their definitions, to build tone and ultimate meaning. Even "man's inventive mind" becomes sinister when followed by the word "brewed" with its associations with witches and mad scientists. Such verbal associations help support Carson's contention that "progress" in insect control has backfired.

The title "Elixirs of Death" provides an ironic introduction to its chapter, linking *elixir*, meaning "life-giving potion" or "cure-all," with death. Chemicals people think helpful, Carson intimates, are proving harmful.

Although she is not often humorous, she uses sarcasm effectively. There were warnings in Great Britain about the dangers of going into arsenic-sprayed fields, she tells us, "but the warning was not understood by the cattle (nor, we must assume, by the wild animals and birds)." When she writes of "a world that is urged to beat its plowshares into spray guns," she introduces a sardonic play on words reversing the biblical injunction to beat swords into plowshares and associating pesticides with warfare.

Carson makes effective use of catalogs, a prose technique used also by poets such as Sandburg and Whitman.

She gives a list of warblers remarkable internal variety and balance, interspersing descriptive phrases between bare names: "the black-and-white, the yellow, the magnolia, and the Cape May; the ovenbird, whose call throbs in the Maytime woods; the Blackburnian, whose wings are touched with flame; the chestnut-sided, the Canadian, and the black-throated green."

As always in her writing, Carson uses grammatical parallels and repeating rhythms to make sentences surge toward a climax. These conclude her description of the consequences of malfunction within the cell: "Then the muscle cannot contract, nor can the impulse race along the nerve pathways. Then the sperm cannot move to its destination; the fertilized egg cannot carry to completion its complex divisions and elaborations."

Cadences suggesting echoes of the King James Bible further dramatize this climax. "If we are going to live so intimately with these chemicals—eating and drinking them, taking them into the very marrow of our bones— we had better know something about their nature and their power." Such verbal suggestions insistently enforce our sense of the importance of her subject, as when she writes "conceived in arrogance," echoing the Declaration of Independence.

"A Fable for Tomorrow," only two pages long, is a particularly rich literary lode that grabs even the casual peruser. Language and form are simple, giving it the aura of a children's story—"So it had been from the days many years ago."

Parallel images and colors emphasize the potential in the idyllic for the catastrophic: "autumn . . . blaze of color that flamed and flickered" is a precursor of "brown and withered vegetation as though swept by fire"; "white clouds of bloom" leads to white powder. DDT has turned the tranquil natural scene into one of devastation. As in a true fable, Carson makes her moral clear: there was no "evil spell"; the people did it themselves.

Carson's images build tone as well as literary effect. She dramatizes her attitude toward the "current vogue for poisons" through a thematic extended metaphor of pesticide use as warfare. When it becomes an article of faith, no longer subject to logical argument, it is a "crusade." Thoughtless use is primitive warfare. In order of appearance:

1. Thus the chemical war is never won, and all life is caught in its violent crossfire.
2. The crusade to create a chemically sterile, insect-free world seems to have engendered a fanatic zeal on the part of many specialists and most of the so-called control agencies.
3. All these [insects] have been our allies in keeping the balance of nature tilted in our favor. Yet we have turned our artillery against our friends.
4. As crude a weapon as the cave man's club, the chemical barrage has been hurled against the fabric of life.

Calling chemical weed killers "a bright new toy," Carson comments that "they give a giddy sense of power over nature to those who wield them," thus integrating the two metaphors so that the use of weed killers is not only warlike but childish.

A graphic simile demonstrates the process of energy production: "The transformation of matter into energy in the cell is an ever-flowing process, one of nature's cycles of renewal, like a wheel endlessly turning." Grains of fuel enter the wheel, go through successive changes, then finally emerge "stripped down," ready to combine with a new molecule and "start the cycle anew."

For more complicated aspects of the process, the wheel image evolves into cell as "chemical factory," with the mitochondria as "powerhouses." Carson graphically warns us that "The crowbar to wreck the wheels of oxidation can be supplied by any of a number of chemicals commonly used as pesticides."

Carson reserves her greatest poetic effect for natural processes or beauty now destroyed, often combining sound devices like alliteration with pronounced mimetic rhythms. Explaining how chemicals spread through the earth's water supply, she writes of "spray that falls directly into streams or that drips down through the leafy canopy to the forest floor, there to become part of the slow movement of seeping moisture beginning its long journey to the sea." Hard consonants, *d*'s, *p*'s and *b*'s, and frequent spondees (single-syllable stressed feet), as in "blizzards drive down," reflect the harsh beauty of life in the "land of the sage."

Interplays of related consonants, as well as straight alliteration, often connect phrases or paragraphs. In the "Fable," the

first *s*ettlers raised their houses, *s*ank their wells, and *b*uilt their *b*arns.

Then a *s*trange *b*light crept over the area.

As in earlier books, background material introduces literary or historical overtones or broadens perspective. A rapid succession of references to Greek mythology—Medea's robe, which brought its wearer violent death—Grimm fairy tales, and Charles Addams's macabre cartoons, suggests that pesticide effects may surpass what we can imagine.

"A house-that-Jack-built sequence, in which the large carnivores had eaten the smaller carnivores, that had eaten the herbivores, that had eaten the plankton, that had absorbed the poison from the water" makes the passage of chemicals through the food chain into a grotesque joke on us.

Robert Frost's poem "The Road Not Taken" gives Carson a chapter title, "The Other Road," and a direct reference, "We stand now where two roads diverge," which she elaborates into the image of our traveling "with great speed" on "a smooth superhighway" with disaster at its end.

The trials of a world filled with pesticides have an

"Alice-in-Wonderland quality" for Carson. She quotes Lewis Carroll with angry humor.

This system, however—deliberately poisoning our food, then policing the result [through government-set maximum permissible amounts, or "tolerances"]—is too reminiscent of Lewis Carroll's White Knight who thought of "a plan to dye one's whiskers green, and always use so large a fan that they could not be seen."

A biblical reference brings not only resonance but ironic reversal when she writes, "By one means or another, the new generations suffer for the poisoning of their parents." New generations suffer not for their parents' sins but for sins visited upon them.

References to "plagues of old" and a brief survey of occurrences of insect disease from "before the time of Aristotle" provide historical perspective. There is another ironic twist when she explains that the use of organic phosphates is an outgrowth of German war work to produce nerve gases.

Some readers object to the highly poetic sections of *Silent Spring*, especially the "Fable," believing that they detract from our sense of Carson's reliability. Careful reading, however, shows that she appropriately qualifies or supports even those sections so as not to be misleading.

John G. Fuller, however, believes that the "Fable" no longer needs qualification. In *The Poison that Fell from the Sky*, he dramatically describes a pesticide accident at a factory in Seveso, Italy, near Milan, where huge quantities of the toxic chemical TCP entered the atmosphere. Beginning his foreword with an adaptation of the "Fable," he italicizes Carson's assurances that the town where all these things have happened does not actually exist. The "Fable," he notes, is "written as a myth, a legend." To critics it is thus "invalid." "The story that follows has changed the myth to a tragic reality, 14 years after *Silent Spring*."[17]

Other readers, particularly contemporary reviewers, praise Carson's writing skills to disparage her science, or express fear that literary brilliance will blind
readers to what these critics consider logical or scientific
flaws. An attack in the London *Economist* begins, "The
American manufacturers of agricultural chemicals . . . in
private . . . are bemoaning the formidable literary powers which have been turned against their insecticides and
pesticides." The reviewer specifically criticizes "her extravagant language."[18]

After referring to her as "the gifted prose-poet-plus
scientist who gave the world 'The Sea Around Us,'" another reviewer comments, "Unfortunately the wonders
she can work with mere words spread her pied-piper's
magic throughout the English-reading world's laity."[19]
Such sentiments no longer enter the world of print, but
surprisingly many scientists and physicians still spout
verbal bias or disparagement, despite abundant proof of
her accuracy and validity.

Anthropologist Loren Eiseley's sympathetic review
closely anticipates most later assessments of *Silent Spring*'s
literary aspects: "If her present book does not possess the
beauty of 'The Sea Around Us,' it is because she has
courageously chosen, at the height of her powers, to ed-
ucate us upon a sad, an unpleasant, an unbeautiful topic,
and one of our own making."[20]

Carson knew *Silent Spring* would evoke criticism and
controversy. It is a highly political book, urging profound
reorientation of beliefs, attitudes, and practices on the
part of both governments and the public. Such sweeping
reassessment threatened the economic interests of powerful corporations and all those they supported in industry, government agencies, and universities. It could
and did lead to governmental actions to control the use
of pesticides.[21]

The book is also highly polemical, intended not
merely to expose facts but to influence decisions. When

Consumers Union published an edition of the book as a "public service project," "the objective" was

to help spread understanding of the major thesis to which Miss Carson's work gives shape: that the public, which must "assume the risks that the insect controllers calculate," must know the facts about those risks before it can decide whether it wishes to continue living with them.

The foreword notes that Carson is "strongly on the *con* side, which very much needs the effective statement it gets here." The book "shatters apathy" and "may help greatly to redress the balance in this area altogether to the public good."[22]

Although recent assessments generally call *Silent Spring* strong but objective, Carson has been charged with bias, sensationalism, and emotionalism. How do such charges stand up to close analysis?

Margery and Lorus Milne, in a review featured on the front page of the *New York Times Book Review*, hit the right balance. "*Silent Spring* is so one-sided that it encourages argument, although little can be done to refute Miss Carson's carefully documented statements."[23]

There is bias. Carson wrote this book with a passion born of her sense of mission. Discussing the validity of claims of wildlife losses after pesticide spraying, she asks, "Which view are we to accept?" When she presents the evidence, however, she clearly indicates her stand: "a record of destruction and death of American wildlife has accumulated."

The London *Economist* accused her of making "propaganda play" with cancer statistics.[24] This charge seems appropriate, but the discussion of cancer statistics is probably the only such example of "playing" with facts in the book. Carson implies that chemicals in the environment have caused an increase in malignant disease, but offers proof only for the increase, not for the causal connection, and even this proof is based on oversimplification of the known facts.

No longer are exposures to dangerous chemicals occupational alone; they have entered the environment of everyone—even of children as yet unborn. It is hardly surprising, therefore, that we are now aware of an alarming increase in malignant disease.

The increase itself is no mere matter of subjective impressions. The monthly report of the Office of Vital Statistics for July 1959 states that malignant growths, including those of the lymphatic and blood-forming tissues, accounted for 15 per cent of the deaths in 1958 compared with only 4 per cent in 1900.

"Alarming increase" was an overstatement. Even now scientists are not certain whether there has been an increase in the incidence of cancer, or in deaths from cancer. The situation is different for different parts of the body, as well as different portions of the population. Lung cancer is increasing, and its close association with smoking has been proven. Acute leukemia in older men is also increasing, but stomach cancer in the United States population as a whole is decreasing. Epidemiologists have changed their statistical base to better take into account underrepresented groups in the population, such as black Americans. This makes comparisons difficult.[25]

Other factors confused the statistical picture in Carson's time, and still do. The incidence of cancer rises significantly after age sixty-five, and there has been a considerable increase in the number of older people in the population. In addition, diagnostic techniques and reporting methods have steadily improved. These elements contribute to higher figures for both the incidence of cancer and cancer deaths. As for the implication that environmental pollutants cause cancer, the evidence is still inconclusive, although there is a good likelihood that some do.

Carson's tone—determined by choice of words and the use of leading rhetorical questions—tends to slant her presentation.

The bitter upland plains, the purple wastes of sage, the wild, swift antelope, and the grouse are then a natural system in perfect balance. Are? The verb must be changed—at least in those already vast and growing areas where man is attempting to improve on nature's way. . . . to satisfy the insatiable demands of the cattleman.

These touches of bitterness, emotional color, and extravagant word choice—"insatiable," for example—lead to charges of emotionalism and sensationalism, which Carson's supporters categorically deny.

Justice William O. Douglas told potential readers, "The alarming story is calmly told, with no theatrics and in a sober, factual way,"[26] but the *Saturday Evening Post* introduced its review, "Thanks to an emotional, alarmist book called *Silent Spring*, . . . Americans mistakenly believe their world is being poisoned."[27]

Ten years later, Shirley Briggs noted "some of the curious charges that *Silent Spring* is an 'emotional' book," commenting that Carson's aim was to bring out in the reader a "shock of recognition and . . . emotions" of the reader's own.[28]

Both supporters and detractors go too far. Carson's scientific accuracy is amply supported in the book itself and has been repeatedly validated, so that those who accuse her of being unscientific or of distorting evidence are off the mark, but it is equally invalid to deny that she uses her own emotions—anger, bitterness—as well as occasional sensationalism, as rhetorical tools to influence readers' emotions.

Carson herself made her intentions clear. She told the Garden Club of America in 1963,

This is a time when forces of a very different nature too often prevail—forces careless of life or deliberately destructive of it and of the essential web of living relationships. . . .

The battle for a sane policy for controlling unwanted species will be a long and difficult one. The publication of *Silent Spring* was neither the beginning nor the end of that struggle.[29]

The book was to be an attack, and after its publication, Carson stayed in the battle to the limits her health allowed. In one speech, she told her audience she was giving "a little inside report from the firing line."[30]

As an exposé of thoughtless practices by both government and industry, *Silent Spring* is in the tradition of the muckraking journalism of such writers as Lincoln Steffens. She veers toward fiction in her opening "Fable" but not to the extent of novels like Upton Sinclair's *The Jungle*, which played a powerful role in cleaning up the meat-packing industry.

Carson presents her muckraking exposé as a powerful "case," with propositions, charges, details, and proofs. Discussing attempts to eradicate the Japanese beetle in Illinois, she charges that authorities (1) do not look at history, citing successful use of natural controls in the East as proof; (2) are shortsighted and misrepresent facts, citing specifics about the cost of using milky spore disease as a natural control, and arguing that it has to be done only once, whereas spraying must be repeated; (3) do not weigh potential disadvantages, such as extraneous destruction and possible harm to humans; and (4) look for "immediate results," even if they do not last.

A syndicated review of the book declares that "She presents her evidence like a public prosecutor, with a relentless battery of testimony."[31] She herself concludes "The Obligation to Endure" with a statement beginning "I contend."

Frank Graham quotes the assessment of Paul B. Sears, Professor Emeritus of Conservation at Yale. "'The result, over and above her usual clarity of structure and presentation, is a brief of which any attorney might well be proud. If anything can convince the court of public opinion, this should do so.'"[32]

What makes *Silent Spring* transcend topical argument and muckraking journalism is that under all the polemics and emotion, with all the facts and narratives, Carson transmits the core of her ecological philosophy. "In each of my books," Carson told the Women's National Book Association, "I have tried to say that all the life of the planet is inter-related, that each species has its own ties to others, and that all are related to the earth. This is the theme of *The Sea Around Us* and the other sea books, and it is also the message of *Silent Spring*."[33]

Immediately after the "Fable," she states her basic philosophical constants: an ecological outlook—"The history of life on earth has been a history of interaction between living things and their surroundings"—intertwined with the perspective of geological time—"Only within the moment of time represented by the present century." Two further elements appear later, the need for further knowledge and a warning of the possible consequences of our thoughtless actions.

When she was called upon to defend *Silent Spring* on the "CBS Reports" television show, "The Silent Spring of Rachel Carson," she restated her concept of our relationship to the "balance of nature" even more cogently.

Now to these people, apparently the balance of nature was something that was repealed as soon as man came on the scene. Well, you might just as well assume that you could repeal the law of gravity. The balance of nature is built of a series of inter-relationships between living things, and between living things and their environment. You can't just step in with some brute force and change one thing without changing a good many others. Now this doesn't mean, of course, that we must never interfere, that we must not attempt to tilt that balance of nature in our favor. But when we do make this attempt, we must know what we're doing, we must know the consequences.[34]

In *Silent Spring* she adds an explicit moral imperative. "Incidents like the eastern Illinois spraying," she writes at the end of "Needless Havoc,"

raise a question that is not only scientific but moral. . . . whether any civilization can wage relentless war on life without destroying itself, and without losing the right to be called civ-

ilized. . . . By acquiescing in an act that can cause such suffering to a living creature, who among us is not diminished as
a human being?

Silent Spring is accepted as an important historical
document, perhaps even a historical monument. It is
mentioned in various lists of seminal books—John Kenneth Galbraith said it changed minds[35]—and included in
lists of epoch-making events of our century. But one reason for its extraordinary effect is its stature as art. Carson
was able to superimpose on her unified scientific presentation the creation of an artistic rhetorical whole.

Reading *Silent Spring* today is an exhilarating but
frightening experience. We know far more about pesticide dangers and have somewhat more control of pesticide use, but the situation is sufficiently unchanged that
the book still serves as a warning and a call to action.

We repeatedly read of nuisances—a bad mosquito
year, gypsy moths spreading through the south—or new
disasters—the litanies of pesticide spills, the legacy of
Agent Orange, the history of Love Canal—that make us
cry, "Rachel Carson warned us this would happen; why
haven't we done something about it?" Yet chemicals are
still introduced into our environment innocent until
proven guilty, as *The New Yorker* described the situation
at Carson's death.[36]

Late in *Silent Spring*, there is a suggested literary
reference that both extends Carson's meaning and links
her message with those of other artists. Commenting on
the results of disrupting oxidation in cells, she uses the
phrase "in men and mice." Literally she is discussing the
relationship between animal experimentation and human
experience, but she is also reversing the phrase borrowed
by American author John Steinbeck from Scottish poet
Robert Burns. The lilt of Carson's line, "in birds and
bacteria, in men and mice," strengthens the suggestion.

Steinbeck often writes of natural processes dis-
rupted. In *The Grapes of Wrath* he portrays the disasters

of the dust bowl brought on by clearing too much land for farming, not unlike what Carson shows happening to the land of the sage, where too much land is being cleared for grazing cattle.

Burns, like Carson, often writes of natural things and reflects profound respect for all life. The final stanzas of "To a Mouse," bring further pungency to Carson's message.

> But, Mousie, thou art no thy lane,
> In proving foresight may be vain:
> The best laid schemes o' mice an' men
> > Gang aft a-gley,
> An' lea'e us nought but grief an' pain
> > For promised joy.
>
> Still thou art blest compared wi' me!
> The present only toucheth thee:
> But oh! I backward cast my e'e
> > On prospects drear!
> An' forward tho' I canna see,
> > I guess an' fear!

The first stanza could well reflect the results of misuse of pesticides, while the second captures the essence of Carson's warning.

Before Rachel Carson published *Silent Spring*, she was a popular author known for both style and substance, but active within a limited range, the sea, its shores, and their inhabitants. After *Silent Spring*, her fame, or to the chemical industry and its supporters, her notoriety, was worldwide. Not only had she produced another bestseller, in an entirely new area, but she had synthesized information never before brought together in one volume. Its impact in her hands was devastating.

~·

7

All of a Piece: Occasional Writings and *The Sense of Wonder*

Rachel Carson surprised many readers with the passion and vehemence of *Silent Spring*. Yet despite this, the attribute that most clearly marks her work is consistency.

No matter what the subject, she never strayed far from her central focus, the interrelationships among human beings, their environment, and other living creatures. From the earliest articles and government pamphlets to *Silent Spring* and the speeches of her final years, her work is all of a piece, with a consistent mission, method, meaning, and message.

Although her first publication, "Undersea" (1937), anticipates *Under the Sea-Wind* in subject matter, many early pieces are land-based, dealing with such subjects as bats and radar (1944), or the usefulness of the starling to human beings (1939).[1] But all of them reflect Carson's enthusiastic appreciation for the mystery and fascination of the natural world.

As part of her job, she wrote fact-filled pamphlets for government publication (1943–1950). Some encouraged housewives to buy unfamiliar local fish to help ease wartime food shortages, while others beautifully introduced national wildlife refuges.[2] Except for two limply pedestrian fish booklets, Carson's government writing has the same lilting grace and evocative descriptions as her commercial work.

Like all her writing, the magazine and government

publications are frankly educational. She serves up attractively presented facts, enriched with intriguing tidbits and permeated by a nutritious philosophical broth calculated to develop healthy attitudes. The starling article counteracts this immigrant bird's unsavory reputation, while "The Bat Knew it First" invites the reader to marvel that nature perfected a version of radar at least sixty million years ago.

In the fish booklets, Carson introduces her "whole-life" approach. She presents underutilized species "as individual creatures—individual in flavor, food values, and gustatory appeal, in their habits, migrations, and relations to a varied sea environment." She believes that if readers have facts, they will act responsibly. "Each of the millions of people who buy and eat fish," she declares, "can play an active part in conservation by utilizing a greater variety of seafoods."[3]

The "Conservation in Action" booklets had multiple purposes: to publicize the wildlife refuges; to act as guidebooks for visitors, enhancing their appreciation of what they saw; and, most important, to engage all readers to fight for the preservation of these critically needed resources. "Wild creatures, like men," each booklet tells us, "must have a place to live." More specifically,

Chincoteague, like other waterfowl refuges, is needed because birds migrate, and because in so doing they expose themselves to great dangers. . . . But while we know little about why birds migrate or how they find their way over enormous distances, common sense tells us this: like human travelers, birds must have places where they can stop in safety for food and rest.[4]

From the first, Carson's writing was rich in controlled artistry and depth of detail. Despite its remarkably abundant information about the sea, its geology and life, all packed into four pages, "Undersea" is lushly written. It opens with a dramatic question and answer.

Who has known the ocean? Neither you nor I, with our earth-bound senses, know the foam and surge of the tide that beats over the crab hiding under the seaweed of his tide-pool home, or the lilt of the long, slow swells of midocean.

There are flowing, rhythmic sentences—"It is water that they breathe, water that brings them food"—and colorful pictures and images—"swarms of diminutive fish twinkle through the dusk like a silver rain of meteors."[5]

Other articles reflect the more pragmatic styles of the magazines that published them. "How about Citizenship Papers for the Starling?" concentrates on details about the starlings' usefulness—they have a voracious appetite for destructive insects such as the Japanese beetle. But Carson begins with a striking historical tidbit. There is no portrait of the starling in John James Audubon's famous *Birds of America*, for there were no starlings in America a century ago. All the uncounted millions here today are descendants of 120 birds imported from Europe in the 1890s.

Carson finds a touch of beauty even in the common starling. She describes "their aerial maneuverings before settling for the night":

In mighty flocks, which grow moment by moment through the addition of new arrivals, they wheel and turn above the buildings, patterning the evening sky with intricate designs. Leaderless, apparently animated by the pure joy of flight, their performance is one of indescribable beauty.[6]

"The Bat Knew it First" has breezy informality. The mother bat hangs her young one "up in good bat fashion by his hind claws on the wall of their cave while she goes ahunting."

Two of the fish booklets are particularly full of imagery and intriguing detail. In "Food from the Sea," we find the vivid picture of "white-meated flounders . . . being brought in . . . by ice-encrusted trawlers from the fishing banks," while later we see "whole schools of young herring . . . washed ashore by storms to silver the beaches with their scales."

Carson enlivens the hake's "biography" by describing how it locates food by touch, dragging its ventral fins on the ground to detect clams or other small animals in the mud. In the booklet on South Atlantic fish, she gives her account of the mullet historical perspective, noting that they "are often mentioned in the writings of the ancient Romans, and in Egypt they have been cultivated for centuries in the overflow deltas of the Nile."[7]

For writing that makes us long to catch the next conveyance of whatever kind to the nearest wildlife refuge, we go to the "Conservation in Action" booklets. "Chincoteague" is rich with sheer loveliness infused with melded wonder and exactness.

Back from the beach the sand mounts into low dunes, and the hills of sand are little by little bound and restrained by the beach grasses and the low, succulent, sand-loving dune plants. As the vegetation increases, the dunes fall away into salt marshes, bordering the bay. Like islands standing out of the low marsh areas are the patches of firmer, higher ground, forested with pine and oak and carpeted with thickets of myrtle, bayberry, sumac, rose, and catbriar.

And:

Up in the marshes around Ragged Point the black ducks have been nesting. In April you might have found their nests here and there under the bayberries; in June the broods of ducklings, with their mothers, begin to appear in the slashes. . . . And early almost any morning of the summer you could see a bittern slinking through the tall salt meadow grass or hear the sharp clatter of the rails.

"Mattamuskeet" shows Carson's sensitivity to the sounds of words: "Mattamuskeet—the rhythmic softness of the Indian name recalls the days when tribes of the Algonquin roamed the flat plains of the coast and hunted game in deep forests of cypress and pine."[8]

Carson always seeks a broad perspective that will help readers sense the long preparation for what we can so quickly destroy: in "Food From the Sea," she tells us that "Iron, copper, magnesium, . . . all essential to human well being, are a few of the minerals that have been accumulating in the sea for thousands of years, washed down from the land by rivers."[9]

The purpose of Carson's government writings demanded a focus on value—nutritive, financial, or recreational—so that we find such uncharacteristic statements as, "From the standpoint of human welfare, thousands upon thousands of pounds of these less known fishes go to waste in the sea each year." But even in these writings, the ecological message is clear. Carson occasionally clothes the ecological with the practical. "We know very little of the life histories of some of the most important species of the region, so that we can only guess how large a fishery they might support."[10]

This enforced emphasis on utility may have influenced *The Sea Around Us*, where Carson not only gives us information about the sea and our relationships with it, but also outlines the practical benefits derived from it. Her discussion of waves, for example, includes the suggestion that learning more about what causes them, and measuring their heights, will help us learn to protect ourselves from unexpected storms and tidal waves.

Near the end of "Undersea" is an early version of Carson's philosophical concept of overriding interrelationships—"Individual elements are lost to view, only to reappear again and again in different incarnations in a kind of material immortality." Shortly before is the intimation of disaster, imminent or accomplished, that so often accompanies ecological statements—Man, she declares, is "Chief, perhaps, among the plunderers."[11]

Such comments are abundant in her conservation writing. "Guarding our Wildlife Resources" begins:

This is the story of the wildlife resources of America, of their place in our history, and their value in our modern life. It is the story of the forces that threaten to destroy them, and the efforts we must make, as individual nations and as a community of nations, to preserve them.

Other pamphlets provide specifics. She describes how "human carelessness" has depleted the population of alewives. As for the birds,

Once there were plenty of natural hostelries for the migrants. That was before our expanding civilization had drained the marshes, polluted the waters, substituted resort towns for wilderness. That was in the days when hunters were few. [12]

An article in *Holiday* magazine in 1958[13] and the preface to the 1961 revised edition of *The Sea Around Us* testify to Carson's growing concern that man was irremediably contaminating the earth.

"Our Ever-Changing Shore" describes the "endless variations" of American coastline. "In every outthrust headland, in every curving beach, in every grain of sand," she tells us, "there is a story of the earth." Carson shares personal experiences in brief word pictures, commenting on the mysterious sublimity of the ocean, that "shining immensity related to far horizons," unaware of man.

Warning readers that natural places are disappearing, she calls for support of National Park Service efforts to bring at least some shore areas under public ownership. National parks alone, however, are not enough. Some land, Carson believes, must be preserved untouched.

In book reviews written earlier in the 1950s, she emphasized the same concerns. Noting Gilbert Klingel's regret that the Chesapeake Bay was losing much that made it unique, she comments,

The truth of this is all too evident to those who have followed the current progress of the bull-dozer and the beach cottage and the hot-dog stand. Perhaps Klingel's book will awaken interest in preserving some of the natural shore areas that are left—places where one can still sense the beauty of the earth and find release from the tensions of our difficult times.[14]

Carson published "Help Your Child to Wonder" in the *Woman's Home Companion* in 1956. She planned to expand the article into a book, but *Silent Spring* preempted the last energies of her working life. After her death, the text of the article was republished as *The Sense of Wonder*, a large-format, glossily attractive book illustrated with large numbers of photographs.

Serene in tone like her earlier work, *The Sense of Wonder* is a culminating statement of Carson's basic philosophy. Her intent was to teach adults how to keep alive a child's sense of wonder while at the same time rediscovering their own sense of the "joy, excitement and mystery of the world we live in."

She uses experiences in Maine with her grandnephew Roger as the basis for instructions as to how we may awaken undeveloped sensitivities to sight, sound, smell, and texture. She and Roger share emotions despite differences in age and experience. Her vivid language is laced with the play of *s*'s and *l*'s as she describes their "same spine-tingling response to the vast roaring ocean": "Together we laughed for pure joy—he a baby meeting for the first time the wild tumult of Oceanus, I with the salt of half a lifetime of sea love in me."

Her style resembles that of a mythic children's tale—"one stormy autumn night"—"just at the edge of where-we-couldn't-see." Waves "that boomed and shouted and threw great handfuls of froth at us" seem like gods, a suggestion reinforced by the reference to Oceanus.

After describing two trips to the ocean edge with Roger, Carson quickly moves to generalize her experiences.

We are continuing that sharing of adventures in the world of nature . . . and I think the results are good. The sharing includes nature in storms as well as calm, by night as well as day, and is based on having fun together rather than on teaching.

She draws us into the world she describes. "I have already promised Roger that we'll take our flashlights this fall and go out into the garden to hunt for the insects that play little fiddles in the grass and among the shrubbery and flower borders." We tour the "living music" of the garden with her, following her extended image of the "insect orchestra," whose sound "swells and throbs night after night, from midsummer until autumn ends and the frosty nights make the tiny players stiff and numb, and finally the last note is stilled in the long cold." For Carson the imaginative response is as valuable as the factual, so that some things, like an unseen creature she calls "the fairy bell ringer," should be left unknown and magical.

Throughout *The Sense of Wonder* Carson's message is clear. We should respond to the natural world with curiosity, delight, awe, and respect. "Ask yourself," she suggests, "What if I had never seen this before? What if I knew I would never see it again?"

We must also respect those with whom we share the world, recognizing both our interdependence and the value and glory of all life. Describing the voices of the birds in spring, she declares, "In that dawn chorus one hears the throb of life itself."

If we are conscious of the sweep of geological time and its ageless elements—"tides rising and falling on their appointed schedule"—we will broaden our perspective and sense of value. Any new perspective, in fact, enhances value by removing what we see from the commonplace. "Aided by a lens, we can escape the limitations of the human size scale."

When Carson explores, she neither interferes nor conquers; she simply reacts. "Piercing the darkness [of the ocean beach] with the yellow cone of our flashlight," Carson and Roger respond to the immensity of nature according to their individual experiences. For her there are "philosophic overtones" in the "sight of . . . small living creatures, solitary and fragile against the brute force of the sea." For Roger, there is "infant acceptance of a world of elemental things," excitement without fear.

She assures parents who do not know the facts of nature as she does that "it is not half so important to *know* as to *feel*." Emotions and sense impressions prepare the soil for the seeds of fact, but "It is possible to compile extensive lists of creatures seen and identified without ever once having caught a breath-taking glimpse of the wonder of life."

In jacket notes written a few years earlier for a recording of *La Mer*, Carson makes a similar point when she appreciatively describes Debussy's "intuitive perception of the mysterious inner nature of the sea, of truths which the science of the ocean, in its infancy in Debussy's time, had not yet discovered."[15]

In the Preface she provided for a booklet, *Humane Biology Projects* (1960), Carson cogently summarizes, in a different context from that in *The Sense of Wonder*, her concept of the value of life.

To understand biology is to understand that all life is linked to the earth from which it came; it is to understand that the stream of life, flowing out of the dim past into the uncertain future, is in reality a unified force, though composed of an infinite number and variety of separate lives.

After commenting on the distortion and sterility of concepts of biology that encourage children to experiment cruelly with living animals, Carson continues:

It is essential that the beginning student should first become acquainted with the true meaning of his subject through observing the lives of creatures in their true relation to each other and to their environment. . . . Only as a child's awareness and reverence for the wholeness of life are developed can his humanity to his own kind reach its full development.[16]

Near the end of *The Sense of Wonder*, Carson asks what the value is "of preserving and strengthening this sense of awe and wonder," of recognizing "something beyond the boundaries of human existence." "Those who dwell, as scientists or laymen, among the beauties and mysteries of the earth," she answers, "are never alone or weary of life." They can find "inner contentment and . . . renewed excitement in living. Those who contemplate the beauty of the earth find reserves of strength that will endure as long as life lasts."

She tells the story of the Swedish oceanographer, Otto Pettersson, who "intensely . . . enjoyed every new experience, every new discovery concerning the world about him." "When he realized he had not much longer to enjoy the earthly scene, Otto Pettersson said to his son: 'What will sustain me in my last moments is an infinite curiosity as to what is to follow.'"

Carson's own philosophy was equally sustaining. Friends marveled at her enthusiastic delight even in continually repeated experiences, like the discovery of a jellyfish on the beach. What seemed to comfort her most at the end of her life was her sense of perspective—it was the "unified force," "the stream of life," that had to be sustained, not the individual life.

Carson accepted the concept of statistical chance. The number of individuals who will survive, under normal conditions, is determined—one or two out of one hundred thousand shad eggs will grow to maturity, she tells us in *Under the Sea-Wind*—but which individuals will survive, and for how long, is subject to random chance. "One dies, another lives. . . ."

The autumn before her death, Carson wrote to a close friend, "When any living thing has come to the end of its cycle, we accept that end as natural. . . . For ourselves . . . it is a natural and not unhappy thing that a life comes to its end." Only rare individuals can apply such concepts with equanimity to their own lives.[17]

After finishing *Silent Spring*, Carson accepted a long-standing invitation to visit Scripps College, in Clare-mont, California. The commencement address[18] she gave there is her valedictory.

She reiterated the major concepts of *Silent Spring*—man's power to conquer nature, his irresponsibility and lack of "wisdom so to control his activities that he would not bring destruction upon himself." Then she added two new notes, one in opposition to established religion, the other to our civilization's fundamental pragmatism.

Attacking "the Jewish-Christian concept of man's relation to nature" that has dominated our thinking, she declared that with "man . . . regarded as the master of all the earth's inhabitants," there "grew the thought that everything on earth—animate or inanimate, animal, veg-etable, or mineral—and indeed the earth itself—had been created expressly for man."

Later in the talk, she asked:

But how is one to assign a value to the exquisite flower-like hydroids reflected in the still mirror of a tide pool? Who can place in one pan of some cosmic scales the trinkets of modern civilization and in the other the song of a thrush in the windless twilight?

So much for pragmatism.

Then she rose to a ringing warning and exhortation.

I used to wonder whether nature—nature in the broadest con-text of the word—actually needed protection from man. Surely the sea was inviolate and forever beyond man's power to change it. Surely the vast cycles by which water is drawn up into the clouds to return again to the earth could never be touched. And just as surely the vast tides of life—the migrating birds—would continue to ebb and flow over the continents, marking the pas-sage of the seasons.

But I was wrong. Even these things, that seemed to belong to the eternal verities, are not only threatened but have already felt the destroying hand of man. . . .

So nature does indeed need protection from man; but man,

too, needs protection from his own acts, for he is part of the living world. His war against nature is inevitably a war against himself. His heedless and destructive acts enter into the vast cycles of the earth, and in time return to him.

Transforming the rhetoric of graduation addresses with the depth of her earnestness and intensity, Carson gave her final peroration.

I wish I could stand before you and say that my own generation had brought strength and meaning to man's relation to nature, that we had looked upon the majesty and beauty and terror of the earth we inhabit and learned wisdom and humility. Alas, this cannot be said, for it is we who have brought into being a fateful and destructive power.

But the stream of time moves forward and mankind moves with it. Your generation must come to terms with the environment. Your generation must face realities instead of taking refuge in ignorance and evasion of truth. Yours is a grave and a sobering responsibility, but it is also a shining opportunity. You go out into a world where mankind is challenged, as it has never been challenged before, to prove its maturity and its mastery—not of nature, but of itself. Therein lies our hope and our destiny. "In today already walks tomorrow."

With consummate grace and integrity, these lines fittingly close the whole of Carson's artistic work.

~·

8

The Artistic Whole

> Life is real! Life is earnest!
> And the grave is not its goal;
> Dust thou art, to dust returnest,
> Was not spoken of the soul.

Henry Wadsworth Longfellow, for all his diminishing reputation, is established as an important nineteenth-century American poet.

Here is Rachel Carson using similar imagery, if from an opposite perspective.

For the sea lies all about us. . . . The continents themselves dissolve and pass to the sea, in grain after grain of eroded land. . . . In its mysterious past it encompasses all the dim origins of life and receives in the end, after, it may be, many transmutations, the dead husks of that same life. For all at last return to the sea.

It is characteristic of the imbalance in Carson's reputation that although many have praised her as a scientist who wrote like a poet, she is not recognized as a significant literary figure, much less given her place in the pantheon of American writers with Henry David Thoreau.

From her earliest occasional writing, through the four major books, to her latest speeches, Carson's work is of a piece in substance, artistry, and underlying philosophy. But even beyond this, her life and work together formed an artistic whole. Preparation, dedication, and her sense of vocation as an artist interlocked with her sense of mission as a moral and social person.

In her life, as in her work, there are balanced rhythmic cycles. She was born inland, and saw the sea for the first time only after graduating from college, but her professional writing began with the sea and returned there repeatedly, even for some of the allusions in *Silent Spring*, just as Carson herself returned each summer to the vacation house she built on the coast of Maine. She began her preparation with literature, turned in fascination to biology, then, responding initially to professional demands that encompassed both, became the scientist as artist.

As naturalist and writer, she is a literary descendant of Thoreau. In personal terms, although they shared a certain reclusiveness, her life seems the opposite of his. Thoreau claimed to have lived the life he "might have writ," even though he did commit many careful words to paper. Carson's life was in her work, except for the part she devoted to her family.

If one keynote of the artistic personality is an overweening belief in the worth of one's art, then Carson was an artist not only in the quality of her work, but in the living of her life. Like all those who choose to be artists rather than pursue easier or more acceptable careers, she had tremendous faith in the importance of her mission and the value of her contributions. Her friend and colleague Shirley Briggs says Carson had "big ideas she wanted people to understand."[1] Accepting their medal in 1952, she told The John Burroughs Society, "In justice not only to ourselves but to the public we ought to develop a more confident and assured attitude toward the role and the value of nature literature."[2]

Carson required discipline and sacrifices from herself, but unlike many artists who expect others to sacrifice their lives to them, Carson expressed warm appreciation for whatever help people might volunteer. Even though she never married, her life reflects a conflict common in women artists, between the need to devote oneself self-absorbedly to work and the compulsion to give of oneself selflessly to family. Three of her books were written under particularly difficult conditions, the first two while working full-time in a demanding editorial position, and the last under the combined pressures of passed deadlines, personal crises, and the burgeoning need for more and more information.

Reviewing Paul Brooks's book about Carson, Irston Barnes recognizes "the vast research that went into both *The Sea Around Us* and *Silent Spring*, the insights that guided her studies, [and] the total immersion in the subject that sustained years of arduous labor."[3]

Her sense of mission reached its climax with *Silent Spring*. She felt compelled to learn all there was to know about pesticides and herbicides, and then to present a synthesis of that knowledge to the public with all the force of her talents and the depth of her ecological perspective.

People have put Rachel Carson into many categories—among them, poet, scientist, conservationist—but these were not separate identities for her. Just as the concept of ecological interrelationships was a cornerstone of her philosophy, so her organizing principle was integration: of interests and activities, occupation and recreation, science and poetry, subject and structure, facts and message. Paul Brooks reports that Carson found his suggestion that she expand her *Holiday* magazine article "into a small book, aimed specifically at saving the rapidly disappearing remnant of unspoiled shoreline. . . . 'an appealing idea, as giving me a chance to *do* something.'"[4]

"I myself am convinced," she told an audience in 1952,

that there has never been a greater need than there is today for

the reporter and interpreter of the natural world. Mankind has
. . . sought to insulate himself, in his cities of steel and concrete,
from the realities of earth and water and the growing seed.
Intoxicated with a sense of his own power, he seems to be going
farther and farther into more experiments for the destruction
of himself and his world.

There is certainly no single remedy for this condition and
I am offering no panacea. But it seems reasonable to believe—
and I do believe—that the more clearly we can focus our attention on the wonders and realities of the universe about us
the less taste we shall have for the destruction of our race.[5]

She saw her obligation as helping others see and
understand. Shirley Briggs writes that "a foray along the
shore or through the spruce woods" with Carson "was
always high adventure. Those of us who had the joy of
sharing some of these expeditions . . . learned much
about the creatures and plants we found, but most of all,
we glimpsed a new way of seeing our world."[6] A century
earlier, Thoreau had written in his journal, "The question is not what you look at, but what you see."[7] We, as
readers, can still share Carson's adventures, and learn to
see.

Carson's major books form changing patterns of
pairs. The first, *Under the Sea-Wind*, and the second, *The
Sea Around Us*, focus on the oceans, while the third, *The
Edge of the Sea*, and the fourth, *Silent Spring*, concentrate
on the land.

The movement from *Under the Sea-Wind* to *The Sea
Around Us* follows the progression of learning experiences
Carson describes in *The Sense of Wonder*, first the emotional, then the intellectual response, with the first preparing the way for the second. In both books, Carson
intended to convey information. In *Under the Sea-Wind*,
facts are integrated into the narratives and thus more
limited, but Carson carefully patterned the content of the
stories to allow logical coverage of the material. Each
story carries us further into the sea until we have reached

the deepest parts and learned about the most complex migrations. In *The Sea Around Us*, the goal of providing information is central, so that orderly presentation of the material determines the form, and geographical coverage is more comprehensive.

From *The Edge of the Sea* to *Silent Spring*, Carson similarly expands both subject matter and geographical coverage, moving from shore areas to the whole of the land, as she moves from an ecological presentation to the dangers of ecological dislocation.

Under the Sea-Wind and *The Edge of the Sea* live on as delightful, informative reading. There is little to become dated and no overt message, although the hints and murmurs are clearly there. These books are literary in character, with her first book taking the narrative approach and her third following the lines of the familiar essay. The first excels in verve and beauty.

The second and fourth books are cosmic in approach, designed to change a reader's perceptions of the world. Filled with facts and emphasizing the latest research, they are highly subject to becoming dated, but Carson's perspective creates a framework for further knowledge. While *The Sea Around Us* is thoroughly objective exposition, leavened with erudite yet intriguing references to history, literature, and myth, *Silent Spring* is an argumentative documentary, thrusting forward facts and interpretations.

In poetic effect, *Under the Sea-Wind* is the highest point on the incline, with the next two books sacrificing some loveliness to the cause of instruction, although the balance remains tilted to the artistic. With its concentration of unpleasant facts, *Silent Spring* is at the lowest point of Carson's poetic writing, yet is still a book of spare beauty with passages of lyrical brilliance.

If someone new to Carson does not want to read all the books in order, it is still best to read *The Sea Around Us* before *Silent Spring*. There is solid support for Carson's later arguments in the earlier book's balanced ecological presentation. A seasoned Carson reader can instantly dismiss *Time*'s ridicule of Carson's contention that pollution of water anywhere leads to contamination everywhere.[8]

Carson saw her work as in the tradition of nature writing. "You have welcomed me into an illustrious company," she told The John Burroughs Society, commenting that the genre "flowered most fully in the works of Richard Jefferies and W. H. Hudson [in England]; . . . in this country the pen of Thoreau—as that of John Burroughs himself—most truly represented the contemplative observer of the world about us."[9]

Although she perfected the scientific approach, she shared themes, preoccupations and literary approaches with naturalist writers of all periods.[10] Nature writers generally use their literary skills to blend information into universal experiences, often working through sense impressions. They seek to awaken wonder, and recognize the need for reverence and love, as well as understanding, stressing the universal urge to live, and the complex web of ecological interrelationships.

Contemporary nature writers increasingly emphasize the impact of human beings on nature. Edwin Way Teale, an important naturalist-writer himself, sees growing interest in "the whole ecological interrelationship of living things," in which "Man, too, is a part of the fabric of nature."[11] Contemporary nature writing as a whole has a tone of deepening forboding, with increasing melancholy and pessimism joining the responses of wonder, joy, kinship, and sympathy.

Like Thoreau and later writers such as critic Joseph Wood Krutch and humorist E. B. White, Carson, in both method and ideas, belongs not only to the line of nature literature, but also to the broader literary tradition. She joins nineteenth-century transcendentalists such as Emerson and Thoreau in the belief that nature provides its own symbols. In her major books, there are the sea

symbols, ranging from the structure of a shell to the
rhythm of the tides. She points out land symbols—migrating birds, seasonal changes—in such works as *The
Sense of Wonder* and a brief piece for *This Week* magazine
called "The Land Around Us."[12]

In chapter 4, I discussed the close resemblance between Carson's ideas in *The Sea Around Us* and those of
eighteenth-century English writers. The same ideas reappear in other books, particularly *The Edge of the Sea*. There
are remarkable similarities between the eighteenth-century concept of "plenitude," the idea that a diverse multitude of living creatures fills every niche in the ascending
"chain of being" leading from the lowest animal forms
to the angels, and Carson's celebration of the abundance
and variety of life and the strength of the life force.

Like eighteenth-century writers and philosophers,
Carson believed that human beings can understand only
a part of the total plan. In both *The Edge of the Sea* and
The Sense of Wonder, she stresses the importance of our
appreciating the mystery and wonder of nature. She
shares also a strong sense of the brevity of human tenancy
of the earth.

In all her books, Carson seeks to undo the common
idea that all things on earth were created for the benefit
of human beings. Alexander Pope disparaged the same
popular notion in the eighteenth century when he wrote:

> Know, Nature's children shall divide her care;
> The fur that warms a monarch warm'd a bear.
> While Man exclaims, "See all things for my use!"
> "See man for mine!" replies a pamper'd goose.

Many modern nature writers similarly encourage
humility. Tomlinson, a writer Carson admired, uses
Pope's brand of ironic humor to make a similar point.

Then, far off, there was a sound, half snarl, half moan. . . . It
was insultingly confident. I had never heard a tiger in his own

place before, and I lost the feeling that man is the noblest work of God; even if he is, perhaps tigers do not know it.[13]

In a recent biography of Joseph Wood Krutch, John Margolis suggests that when Krutch wrote about Thoreau, a strong influence on him, he also described his own attitudes. Krutch's description applies to Carson as well.

Thoreau, Krutch said, moved "away from the transcendental assumption that the meaning of nature can be reached by intuition and toward the fundamentally scientific assumption—namely, that only through observation may one ultimately reach not merely dead facts but those which understanding can make live."

Intellectual understanding alone was useless for Thoreau without "'that warm and sympathetic sense of oneness.'" For both Thoreau and Krutch, Margolis concludes, the "distinctive quality" of the experience with the natural object was shared delight.[14]

Carson often wrote about her literary likes and influences. She told readers how she kept Thoreau's journals and Jefferies' nature essays near her bed, often reading them to relax before going to sleep.[15] In addition to its informational references, *The Sea Around Us* includes a list of great sea books. While it was on the best-seller list, Carson also published newspaper articles like "A Treasure Chest of Sea Books" and "Sea Leaves its Mark on World Poets." After praising Conrad for his magnificent descriptions of waves, wind, and water, she writes of Melville's *Moby Dick*, "Apart from its symbolism and human significance, it is a portrayal of the sea that in concept and execution stands apart from all others," reflecting "the timeless, unhurried spirit of the sea." Among modern sea writers, she celebrates H. M. Tomlinson and Henry Beston.

Carson includes Masefield, Shakespeare, Coleridge, Shelly, Keats, and the old English author of "The Seafarer" among poets for whom the sea was an inspiration and theme, but saves her greatest enthusiasm for Swinburne, who captured the sea's "very essence . . . in his rhythmic flow of words," giving us "in verse something of the hypnotic effect of the sea itself."[16]

She often named Henry Williamson and Henry Beston as authors who particularly influenced her. Her use of animals like Scomber the mackerel as central figures in *Under the Sea-Wind* resembles Williamson's treatment of his animals in *Tarka the Otter*, while the rhythm and flow of much of her writing is like Beston's cadences in *The Outermost House*. In a section called "The Headlong Wave," Beston captures the sounds of the surf, then moves into a sweeping perspective: "Night and day, age after age, so works the sea, with infinite variation obeying an unalterable rhythm moving through an intricacy of chance and law."[17]

Beston too had exacting verbal standards. His wife writes that he "observed carefully, brooded long, and wrote slowly." "He never typed, for the sound of a machine would have interfered with the rhythm of his sentences, which meant so much to him." Words and cadence . . . [were] equally important."[18]

Although there are facts to support Beston's minutely detailed descriptions, he emphasizes his own reactions, seeking the larger picture, but seemingly unconcerned with transmitting information or particular messages. Only the texture of Carson's writing resembles his—the attention to rhythm, sounds, word choices, and techniques, and the skillful blend of literary and historical references. This passage from *The Outermost House* may have suggested Carson's insect-orchestra metaphor in *The Sense of Wonder*: "But all those little fiddles in the grass, all those cricket pipes, those delicate flutes, are they not lovely beyond words when heard in midsummer on a moonlight night?"[19]

Carson's references to nature's symbols may be

closer to John Muir's transcendentalism than to the earlier, more literal version of Thoreau. Muir, a conservationist who played a crucial role in the founding of America's national parks, did not pretend to understand nature's meaning.

The night wind is telling the wonders of the upper mountains, their snow fountains and gardens, forests and groves; even their topography is in its tones. . . . The horizon is bounded and adorned by a spiry wall of pines, every tree harmoniously related to every other; definite symbols, divine hieroglyphics written with sunbeams. Would I could understand them![20]

Carson differs from most nature writers in the solidity of her scientific base. When she generalizes, she bases her statements directly on specific facts or personal explorations. She always integrates the beauty of her medium and her literary techniques with the scenes or situations that call them forth, avoiding abstract rhapsodies and emotional tangents.

U.S. Secretary of the Interior Stewart Udall's tribute to Rachel Carson, a month after her death, shows, in the attributes he praised and the order he imposed on them, how successfully Carson joined science and literature, nature writing and poetry. She combined "the scientist's eye and the poet's sense," Udall writes.

And the lyric tone of her prose, the insights she drew from her research, her clear commitment to nature's scheme of things made her a memorable teacher. There was always, there to admire in her work, the effortless way with which she bridged the gap between science and the humanities.[21]

Carson's own statements frequently give us insight into her values. Reading her comment that "Poets often have a perception that gives their words the validity of science," we realize that for her, science carried the most weight.[22] She clarified her approach in a statement for *Twentieth Century Authors*. "As a writer, my interest is divided between the presentation of facts and the interpretation of their underlying significance, with emphasis, I think, toward the latter."[23]

As for style, she always screened her writing for "passages where disharmonies of sound might distract attention from the thought." Critically reviewing a less careful author, she complains, "Often it is difficult to hear what the author is saying because of the tumult of verbs at war with their subjects, and of 'sentences' that are only a confused tangle of phrases lacking sometimes a subject, sometimes a predicate."[24]

Value, for Carson, was not measured by number of facts. She criticized one writer who "managed to compress 5,000 years of undersea history" into a book of only moderate size, concluding that "the very multiplicity of facts and the terse style in which they are presented are somewhat detrimental to the reading qualities of the book."[25]

In two glowing book reviews, Carson suggests her own goals. Calling attention to Gilbert Klingel's awareness of all the senses and his rich imagery and evocative descriptions, Carson praises his "ability to describe the life of a limited area in terms that invest it not only with fascination but with rich meaning." Above all, "the universal themes of the slow unfolding of earth history and of the ceaseless, incomprehensible struggle of life to survive and to perpetuate itself . . . flow from a solid foundation of carefully observed fact."[26]

She believes Jacquetta Hawkes achieves the "happy union of scientist and creative artist." "And out of the materials of these sciences her richly creative mind has evoked an image of 'an entity, the land of Britain, in which past and present, nature, man, and art appear all in one piece.' Such a book leaves the reader vastly richer not only in information but in understanding. It is always a joy to come in contact with a mind at once informed with scientific fact and leavened with imagination and intuitive understanding." She tells us to read Hawkes's book both for facts and for "deeper significance in interpreting the relation of man to his environment."[27] We know she wants us to read her own books the same way.

If we compare a recent book by Robert van den Bosch, *The Pesticide Conspiracy*,[28] with *Silent Spring*, we see the basis of *Silent Spring*'s success. Van den Bosch believes the chemical industry, the government, and those working with them, conspire against other approaches to pest control. He calls his prologue "Silent Spring Revisited." There are insects and birds, but man has wiped himself out. "A fable?," van den Bosch asks. "Lets [sic] talk about it."

His writing has none of *Silent Spring*'s awesome prophetic quality. It is overloaded with explosive adjectives—"corruptive, coercive and sinister"—with jargon, and with superlatives, all of which destroy his credibility. He limits his approach by appealing only to man's selfish interest in man. Writing about the results of interference with nature, he provides insufficient particulars and inadequate documentation. Although Van den Bosch is a respected professor and researcher, he springs all the traps Carson avoids.

"No writer can stand still," Carson told the American Association of University Women in 1956. "Each task completed carries its own obligation to go on to something new."[29] When she died, she left many projects uncompleted—the "Help Your Child to Wonder" book, the important book on man and the environment, the war against unwise use of pesticides.

Nonetheless, the four books she wrote, and the scattering of pamphlets and articles, are a substantial accomplishment. A *New York Times* editorial eloquently testifies to Carson's place in history.

She was a biologist, not a crusader, but the power of her knowledge and the beauty of her language combined to make Rachel Carson one of the most influential women of our time.

For years warnings had been sounded about the lethal effects on wildlife—and possibly on human life—of the indiscriminate use of poisonous chemical sprays. But it was not until the publication of Miss Carson's "Silent Spring" in 1962 that the entire nation was alerted to the hazards to man and nature caused by pesticides.[30]

Silent Spring began as an exposé of the dangers of pesticides but came close to becoming the major ecological work Carson had wanted to write. As in all her work, style and structure relate organically to the particular subject, but *Silent Spring* is nonetheless an extension of the motifs and themes of earlier books. When Douglas Costle, as Administrator of the United States Environmental Protection Agency, declared that Rachel Carson "sounded the alarm about environmental dangers," he credited not *Silent Spring* alone, but "her unique, empathetic presentation of the workings of nature in *Under the Sea-Wind, The Sea Around Us, The Edge of the Sea*, and finally *Silent Spring*."[31]

Before the publication of *Silent Spring*, Carson's audience was smaller, but her reputation already considerable. As early as 1944, the respected scientist and writer William Beebe had included some of *Under the Sea-Wind* in *The Book of Naturalists, An Anthology of the Best Natural History*.[32] The book jacket of Edwin Way Teale's *Green Treasury* of 1952 had described its range of selections as "From Marco Polo telling of the fabulous falcons of Kublai Khan to Rachel L. Carson writing of the sea."

Her claim to a place in literature as well as history rests on all her books, each an individually realized achievement representing a different kind of writing, all testifying that she possessed what William Beebe considered the "*ideal* equipment for a naturalist writer of literary natural history":

Supreme enthusiasm, tempered with infinite patience and a complete devotion to truth; the broadest possible education; keen eyes, ears, and nose; the finest instruments; opportunity for observation; thorough training in laboratory technique;

comprehension of known facts and theories, and the habit of giving full credit for these in the proper place; awareness of what is not known; ability to put oneself in the subject's place; interpretation and integration of observations; a sense of humor; facility in writing; an eternal sense of humbleness and wonder. [33]

This is Rachel Carson.

Under the Sea-Wind best shows her empathy with the creatures of the sea and the literary flair and abundant grace with which she spins her stories. *The Sea Around Us*, as another anthologist rhapsodized, "introduced thousands of people to the fascination of one of the most familiar but least-known areas on the surface of the globe—the ocean. It also introduced thousands of people to some extraordinarily beautiful nature writing." [34] It is a thorough treatise on the geology, history, biology, ecology, and economics of the sea, and more, but Carson's "supreme enthusiasm," and all the other attributes Beebe lists, make it the masterpiece it is.

In *The Edge of the Sea* and *The Sense of Wonder*, Carson is relaxed and openly philosophical. She speaks to us directly so that we share delightful educational explorations, learning not only what nature means to Carson but what it can mean for us and for the children who explore with us. Reading these two books, we nestle in valleys below Carson's impressive literary peaks, but no visit to the coast is the same after *The Edge of the Sea*, and no woodland stroll or moonlit wanderings on the beach fail to remind us of our "sense of wonder."

Whenever pesticide problems or other ecological issues come to public attention, Rachel Carson is cited and honored. She even appears on a postage stamp. Perhaps the best proof of her lively presence is that she is still criticized, still controversial.

Henry David Thoreau is credited with making the nature essay a literary form. Rachel Carson has done the same for the science book. Her work is not yet recognized as the beginning of a new literary tradition, but its influence may already have affected the best recent science books for the general public.

Carson's example is hard to follow. It takes major talent to turn science into poetry. But when science writers pay attention to the craft of their writing, treating it as literary art, when they seek the broad perspective as well as the accurate statement, science writing can become literature. Each of Carson's books seems so distinct from the others that it is difficult to see them as representing a single departure in tradition, but it is their common strengths in form, tone, perspective, and style that make them so readable, and thus so effective as both science and literature.

When we look closely at Carson's subtle layers of meaning, when we measure her aesthetic effect and philosophical impact, we know that Rachel Carson is a preeminent writer of nonfiction. We know that she belongs not only in history, but in literary history as well. With seeming ease and fluent grace, her books fulfill the classic aims of literature, to teach and to delight.

Notes

1. SCIENTIST AS ARTIST

1. Rachel Carson, "Design for Nature Writing, Remarks made on Acceptance of the John Burroughs Medal, April 7, 1952," Rachel Carson papers, Rachel Carson Council (formerly Rachel Carson Trust for the Living Environment), Washington, D.C.
2. Rachel Carson, "National Book Award Acceptance Speech," in Paul Brooks, *The House of Life: Rachel Carson at Work* (Boston: Houghton Mifflin, 1972), p. 128.
3. "The Gentle Storm Center," *Life*, 12 October 1962, p. 105.
4. Carson to Ruth Nanda Anshen, 7 January 1956, in Brooks, *House of Life*, p. 2.

2. NATURE AND BOOKS

1. Information on Maria McLean Carson and Rachel Carson's early home environment is from Philip Sterling's book for juveniles, *Sea and Earth: The Life of Rachel Carson* (New York: Thomas Y. Crowell, 1970), pp. 6–35. Paul Brooks, *The House of Life: Rachel Carson at Work* (Boston: Houghton Mifflin, 1972) provides the best sense of Rachel Carson as a person through extensive quotations from her letters and other previously unpublished writings.
2. Margaret Fifer, "I Remember Rachel," read to Pittsburgh Poetry Society, 13 April 1973, unpublished typescript, Rachel Carson papers, Rachel Carson Council (formerly

Rachel Carson Trust for the Living Environment), Washington, D.C., p. 9.

3. Stanley J. Kunitz, ed., *Twentieth Century Authors*, First Supplement (New York: H. W. Wilson, 1955), p. 174.

4. Dorothy Thompson Seif, "The Legacy of Rachel Carson—Wonder, Awareness, and Warning: Pennsylvania College for Women 1928–29," unpublished typescript, Rachel Carson papers, Rachel Carson Council, p. 4.

5. Carson to Dorothy Freeman, 12 March 1963, in Brooks, *House of Life*, p. 319.

6. Kunitz, *Twentieth Century Authors*, p. 174.

7. Rachel Carson, Autobiographical Sketch in *New York Herald Tribune Book Review*, 7 October 1951, p. 4.

8. David McCord, review of *House of Life* by Paul Brooks, *Saturday Review*, 25 March 1972, p. 109.

9. Carson, Autobiographical Sketch, p. 4.

10. "The Gentle Storm Center," *Life*, 12 October 1962, p. 106.

11. Carson to Marjorie Spock, 4 December 1958, in Brooks, *House of Life*, p. 242.

12. Brooks, *House of Life*, p. 8.

13. Ibid., p. 117.

14. Interview with Shirley A. Briggs, Bethesda, Md., 20 July 1979.

15. Brooks, *House of Life*, p. 17.

16. Frank Graham, Jr., *Since Silent Spring* (Boston: Houghton Mifflin, 1970), p. 11.

17. Sterling, *Sea and Earth*, p. 34.

18. Fifer, "I Remember Rachel," p. 4.

19. Carson to Dorothy Thompson [Seif], 24 August 1931, Rachel Carson papers, Rachel Carson Council.

20. Brooks, *House of Life*, p. 242.

21. Interview with Dorothy Algire, Bethesda, Md., 20 July 1979, and quotation from secretary in Lillian Moore, "Rachel Carson's 'Silent Spring'—its Truth and its Influence Go Marching On and On," *Smithsonian* 1 (July 1970): 6.

22. Kunitz, *Twentieth Century Authors*, p. 174.

23. Carson to Mary Frye, 20 March 1928 and 6 August 1928, Rachel Carson papers, Rachel Carson Council.

24. Carson to Dorothy Thompson [Seif], 25 August 1929, Rachel Carson papers, Rachel Carson Council.

25. Interview with Shirley A. Briggs, 19 July 1979.

26. Shirley A. Briggs, "Remembering Rachel Carson," *American Forests* 76 (July 1970): 10.

27. Rachel L. Carson, "The Bat Knew It First," *Collier's*, 114 (18 November 1944): 24.

28. Brooks, *House of Life*, p. 75.

29. Rachel L. Carson, "Undersea," *Atlantic Monthly* 160 (1937): 322–25; reprinted in Brooks, *House of Life*, pp. 22–29.

30. "Contributor's Column," *Atlantic Monthly* 160 (1937): n.p.

31. Carson, "Undersea," p. 325.

32. Ibid., p. 323.

33. William Beebe, review of *Under the Sea-Wind* by Rachel Carson, *Saturday Review*, 27 December 1941, p. 5.

34. William Beebe, *The Book of Naturalists: An Anthology of the Best Natural History* (New York: Alfred A. Knopf, 1944).

35. Brooks, *House of Life*, p. 127.

36. *New York Times*, 15 April 1964, p. 25.

37. Seif, "Legacy of Rachel Carson," p. 20.

38. Interview with Briggs, 19 July 1979.

39. Frank Graham, Jr., "Rachel Carson," *EPA Journal*, 4 (1978): 6–7.

40. Many examples in Brooks, *House of Life*.

41. Interview with Briggs, 19 July 1979.

42. Rachel Carson, Address to Theta Sigma Phi, 21 April 1954, in Brooks, *House of Life*, p. 132.

43. "Gentle Storm Center," p. 105.

44. Carson to Lois Crisler, 28 November 1963, in Brooks, *House of Life*, pp. 321–22.

45. Brooks, *House of Life*, p. 302.

46. Rachel Carson, *The Sea*, ed. Vesey-Fitzgerald (London: MacGibbon & Kee, 1964), p. vii.

47. Graham, *Since Silent Spring*, p. 9.

48. Rachel Carson, "Help Your Child to Wonder," *Woman's Home Companion*, 83 (July 1956): 2–7+.

49. Rachel Carson, "Our Ever-Changing Shore," *Holiday*, 24 (July 1958): 71, 117–20; reprinted in Brooks, *House of Life*, pp. 216–26.

50. Graham, *Since Silent Spring* and Brooks, *House of Life* both thoroughly cover the genesis and development of *Silent Spring*, Graham in the context of the use, abuse, and control of pesticides, and Brooks as part of his account of Carson's intellectual life.

51. Graham, *Since Silent Spring*, p. 32.

52. Ibid., p. 34.

53. Brooks, *House of Life*, p. 271.

54. Graham, *Since Silent Spring*, p. 36.

55. Rachel Carson, "Of Man and the Stream of Time" (commencement address, Scripps College, Claremont, Calif., 1962), Scripps College *Bulletin*, July 1962, pp. 5–6 (offprint supplied through the courtesy of the college).

56. Rachel Carson, speech to Women's National Press Club, 5 December 1962, in Brooks, *House of Life*, p. 302.

57. *Time*, 24 April 1964, p. 73.

58. Interview with Briggs, 19 July 1979.

59. Brooks, *House of Life*, p. 270.

60. Carson to Crile, 7 December 1960, Rachel Carson papers, Rachel Carson Council.

61. Interview with Briggs, 20 July 1979.

62. Ann Cottrell Free, "The Opening of the Door," *Defenders of Wildlife News* 47 (September 1972): 345.

63. Carson, Autobiographical Sketch, p. 4.

64. Communication to members, Rachel Carson Council, August 1980.

3. LIVES IN THE SEA: *UNDER THE SEA-WIND*

1. Paul Brooks, *The House of Life: Rachel Carson at Work* (Boston: Houghton Mifflin, 1972), pp. 5–6.

2. Joseph Wood Krutch, *The Best of Two Worlds* (New York: William Sloane Associates, 1953), pp. 92–94. Walter John Herrscher discusses Krutch's attitudes in the context of those of other nature writers in "Some Ideas in Modern American Nature Writing" (Ph.D. dissertation, University of Wisconsin, 1969), pp. 179–81.

3. Brooks, *House of Life*, p. 6.

4. Rachel Carson, "The Land Around Us," *This Week* (mag-

azine section of the *New York Herald Tribune* and other newspapers), 25 May 1952.

5. William Beebe, *The Book of Naturalists: An Anthology of the Best Natural History* (New York: Alfred A. Knopf, 1944).

6. William Beebe, review of *Under the Sea-Wind* by Rachel Carson, *Saturday Review*, 27 December 1941, p. 5.

7. Frank Graham, Jr., *Since Silent Spring* (Boston: Houghton Mifflin, 1970), p. 6.

8. Beebe, review, p. 5.

9. David McCord, review of *The House of Life* by Paul Brooks, *Saturday Review*, 25 March 1972, p. 108.

10. A. C. Spectorsky, ed., *The Book of the Sea* (New York: Grosset & Dunlap, 1954), p. 290.

11. Interview with Dorothy Algire, Bethesda, Md., 20 July 1979; Brooks, *House of Life*, p. 35; Rachel Carson, *The Sea*, ed. Brian Vesey-Fitzgerald (London: MacGibbon & Kee, 1964), p. viii.

4.   RETURN TO OCEANUS: *THE SEA AROUND US*

1. Application for Eugene F. Saxton Fellowship, 1949, Rachel Carson collection, Beinecke Library, Yale University.

2. Rachel Carson, Autobiographical Sketch, *New York Herald Tribune Book Review*, 7 October 1951, p. 4.

3. Rachel Carson collection, Beinecke Library. All references to Carson's notes or manuscripts pertain to this collection.

4. Paul Brooks, *The House of Life: Rachel Carson at Work* (Boston: Houghton Mifflin, 1972), p. 128.

5. Jonathan Norton Leonard, "—And his Wonders in the Deep, A Scientist Draws an Intimate Portrait of the Winding Sea and Its Churning Life," *New York Times Book Review*, 1 July 1951, p. 1.

6. Alexander Pope, "An Essay on Man," Epistle 1, line 60.

7. Joseph Addison, "On the Scale of Being," *The Spectator*, no. 519, 25 October 1712.

8. Pope, "Essay on Man," 1, lines 35–36.

9. Ibid., line 72.

10. Bonamy Dobrée, *English Literature in the Early Eighteenth Century* (New York and London: Oxford University Press, 1959), p. 28.

11. Pope, "Essay on Man," 1, line 294.

12. Dobrée, *English Literature*, pp. 541–46.

13. Walter Sullivan, "Depths Off Ecuador Yield Clues to Life," *The New York Times*, 15 July 1979, I, p. 9.

14. Edwin Way Teale, *Green Treasury, A Journey Through the World's Great Nature Writing* (New York: Dodd, Mead, 1952), p. 28.

15. A. C. Spectorsky, ed., *The Book of the Sea* (New York: Grosset & Dunlap, 1954), pp. ix–x.

16. Rachel Carson, "The Birth of an Island," *Yale Review*, September 1950.

5.   EMERGING FROM THE SEA: *THE EDGE OF THE SEA*

1. Paul Brooks, *The House of Life: Rachel Carson at Work* (Boston: Houghton Mifflin, 1972), p. 153.

2. Brooks, *House of Life*, p. 152.

3. Walter John Herrscher, "Some Ideas in Modern American Nature Writing" (Ph.D. dissertation, University of Wisconsin, 1969), p. 120, discusses this concept as expressed by Aldo Leopold, particularly in *Round River* (1953), in the context of other nature writing.

4. Brooks, *House of Life*, pp. 158–59.

5. Brooks, *House of Life*, p. 163, note p. 335.

6. Jonathan N. Leonard, "Between the Mark of High Tide and Low," *New York Times Book Review*, 30 October 1955, p. 5.

7. Fanny Butcher, *Chicago Sunday Tribune*, 30 October 1955, p. 3.

8. Robert Cushman Murphy, *New York Herald Tribune Book Review*, 30 October 1955, p. 3.

9. *Time*, 7 November 1955, p. 128.

6.   A BOOK FOR OUR TIME: *SILENT SPRING*

1. Rachel Carson, "What's the Reason Why: A Symposium by Best-Selling Authors," *New York Times Book Review*, 2 December 1962, p. 3.

2. James Whorton, *Before Silent Spring: Pesticides and Public Health in Pre-DDT America* (Princeton, N.J.: Princeton University Press, 1974); Frank Graham, Jr., *Since Silent Spring* (Boston: Houghton Mifflin, 1970).

3. Whorton, *Before Silent Spring*, pp. vii, 253.

4. Harry Scherman, *Book-of-the-Month Club News*, September 1962, p. 1.

5. Paul Brooks, *The House of Life: Rachel Carson at Work* (Boston: Houghton Mifflin, 1972), p. 229. See chapter 2 for more thorough coverage. Both Brooks and Graham present detailed accounts of the events leading Carson to write *Silent Spring* and the difficult period of research and writing.

6. Ibid., p. 228.

7. Carson to Paul Brooks, in ibid., p. 237; ibid., p. 239.

8. Ibid., pp. 243–44.

9. Shirley A. Briggs, "A Decade After Silent Spring," *Friends Journal*, 1 March 1972, p. 148.

10. Brooks, *House of Life*, p. 263.

11. Rachel Carson collection, Beinecke Library, Yale University.

12. Dr. Janet Rowley, Department of Medicine, University of Chicago, to the author, 1 July 1981.

13. Elizabeth C. Miller and James A. Miller, "Mechanisms of Chemical Carcinogenesis," *Cancer* 47 (1 March 1981): 1055.

14. Ibid., abstract, p. 1055.

15. Hyman J. Zimmerman, M.D., *Hepatotoxicity: The Adverse Effects of Drugs and other Chemicals on the Liver* (New York: Appleton-Century-Crofts, 1978), pp. 334–35. All references to Zimmerman are from chapter 15, "The Hepatotoxic Potential of a Polluted Environment," pp. 333–45.

16. David Schottenfeld, M.D., "The Epidemiology of Cancer: An Overview," *Cancer* 47 (1 March 1981): 1106.

17. John G. Fuller, *The Poison that Fell from the Sky* (New York: Berkley [by arrangement with Random House], 1977), foreword.

18. Review of *Silent Spring*, (London) *Economist*, 20 October 1962, pp. 248, 251.

19. Hermann Deutsch, "Pesticide Volume Pushes 'Panic Button'," *New Orleans States-Item*, 28 November 1962.

20. Loren Eiseley, review of *Silent Spring*, *Saturday Review* 45 (29 September 1962): 18.

21. For a fuller account of the controversy that greeted *Silent Spring* and its author, see chapter 2; information also in Brooks, *House of Life*, and Graham, *Since Silent Spring*.

22. Rachel Carson, *Silent Spring* (Boston: Houghton Mifflin, 1962), Special Edition for *Consumer Reports* Subscribers Only, pp. xi–xii.

23. Lorus and Margery Milne, "There's Poison All Around Us Now; The Dangers in the Use of Pesticides are Vividly Pictured by Rachel Carson," *New York Times Book Review*, 23 September 1962, p. 26.

24. (London) *Economist* review, p. 248.

25. Dr. Janet Rowley to the author, 30 July 1981; Schottenfeld, "Epidemiology," pp. 1095–96.

26. William O. Douglas, *Book-of-the-Month Club News*, September 1962, p. 2.

27. Edwin Diamond, "The Myth of the 'Pesticide Menace'," *Saturday Evening Post* 236 (28 September 1963): 16.

28. Briggs, "Decade," pp. 148–49.

29. "From Rachel Carson's manuscript of the talk to the Garden Club of America, New York City, January 8, 1963 upon receiving the GCA Special Commendation," typescript, Rachel Carson Council (formerly Rachel Carson Trust for the Living Environment), Washington, D.C., p. 1.

30. "Address by Dr. Rachel Carson at Audubon Dinner, 5 October 1962," typescript, Rachel Carson Council, p. 2. There are many typescripts of speeches and congressional testimony both in the Rachel Carson collection at the Beinecke Library of Yale University and at the Rachel Carson Council.

31. Miles A. Smith, review of *Silent Spring*, Bristol, Conn. *Press* and other newspapers, Rachel Carson collection, Beinecke Library.

32. Graham, *Since Silent Spring*, p. 63.

33. Ibid., p. 53.

34. "CBS Reports": "The Silent Spring of Rachel Carson,"

transcript of broadcast over the CBS Television Network, Wednesday, 3 April 1963, 7:30–8:30 P.M. E.S.T., p. 30, Rachel Carson collection, Beinecke Library.

35. "Immortal Nominations," *New York Times Book Review*, 3 June 1979, p. 13:

The Book Review asked a number of writers the following: Which post–World War II books have already established themselves or may eventually establish themselves in a group of a hundred or so of the most important books of Western literature; also, which prewar books that were not considered in this category might now be, in light of the history of the last three decades?

36. "Notes and Comment," *New Yorker* 40 (2 May 1964): 35.

7. ALL OF A PIECE: OCCASIONAL WRITINGS AND *THE SENSE OF WONDER*

1. Rachel L. Carson, "Undersea," *Atlantic Monthly*, 160 (1937): 322–25 (reprinted in Paul Brooks, *The House of Life: Rachel Carson at Work* [Boston: Houghton Mifflin, 1972], pp. 22–29); "The Bat Knew it First," *Collier's* 114 (1944): 24; and "How About Citizenship Papers for the Starling?" *Nature* 32 (1939): 317–19.

2. Rachel L. Carson, *Conservation Bulletins* 33, 34, 37, and 38: "Food from the Sea: Fish and Shellfish of New England" (Washington, D.C.: U.S. Government Printing Office, 1943); "Food from Home Waters: Fishes of the Middle West" (Washington, D.C.: U.S. Government Printing Office, 1943); "Fish and Shellfish of the South Atlantic and Gulf Coasts" (Washington, D.C.: U.S. Government Printing Office, 1944); and "Fish and Shellfish of the Middle Atlantic Coast" (Washington, D.C.: U.S. Government Printing Office, 1945). Conservation in Action, Numbers 1, 2, 4, 5, and 8: "Chincoteague, A National Wildlife Refuge" (Washington, D.C.: U.S. Government Printing Office, 1947); "Parker River, A National Wildlife Refuge" (Washington, D.C.: U.S. Government Printing Office, 1947); "Mattamuskeet, A National Wildlife Re-

fuge" (Washington, D.C.: U.S. Government Printing Office, 1947); "Guarding Our Wildlife Resources" (Washington, D.C.: U.S. Government Printing Office, 1948); and, with Vanez T. Wilson, "Bear River, A National Wildlife Refuge" (Washington, D.C.: U.S. Government Printing Office, 1950).

3. Carson, "Food from the Sea," verso of title page and pp. 1–2.
4. Carson, "Chincoteague," verso of title page and p. 1.
5. Carson, "Undersea," p. 322.
6. Carson, "Starling," p. 318.
7. Carson, "Food from the Sea," pp. 6, 19, 38, and "Fish and Shellfish of the South Atlantic," p. 10.
8. Carson, "Chincoteague," pp. 2, 11; "Mattamuskeet," p. 1.
9. Carson, "Food from the Sea," p. 5.
10. Ibid., p. 2; "Fish and Shellfish of the South Atlantic," p. 3.
11. Carson, "Undersea," pp. 325, 323.
12. Carson, "Food from the Sea," p. 16; "Guarding our Wildlife Resources," p. 1; "Chincoteague," p. 1.
13. Carson, "Our Ever-Changing Shore," *Holiday* 24 (1958): 71, 117–20; reprinted in Brooks, *House of Life*, pp. 216–26.
14. Rachel L. Carson, "The Dark Green Waters" (review of Gilbert C. Klingel, *The Bay*), *New York Times Book Review*, 14 October 1951, p. 20.
15. Rachel L. Carson, record jacket notes, Debussy, *La Mer*, RCA Victor, LM 1221, 1951.
16. Rachel L. Carson, "To Understand Biology," included in article by Shirley A. Briggs, Audubon Naturalist Society, offprint in Rachel Carson papers, Rachel Carson Council (formerly Rachel Carson Trust for the Living Environment), Washington, D.C.
17. Carson to Dorothy Freeman, 10 September 1963, in Brooks, *House of Life*, pp. 326–27.
18. Rachel Carson, "Of Man and the Stream of Time" (commencement address, Scripps College, Claremont, Calif., 1962), Scripps College *Bulletin*, July 1962 (offprint supplied through the courtesy of the college).

8.   THE ARTISTIC WHOLE

1. Interview with Shirley Briggs, 19 July 1979.
2. Rachel L. Carson, "Design for Nature Writing, Remarks
    made on Acceptance of the John Burroughs Medal, April
    7, 1952," Rachel Carson papers, Rachel Carson Council
    (formerly Rachel Carson Trust for the Living Environ-
    ment), Washington, D.C.
3. Irston R. Barnes, "Rachel Carson at Work" (review of
    Paul Brooks, *The House of Life: Rachel Carson at Work*, *The
    Naturalist*, 26 March 1972, p. 2.
4. Paul Brooks, *House of Life* (Boston: Houghton Mifflin,
    1972), p. 214.
5. Carson, "Design."
6. Shirley A. Briggs, "The Rachel Carson National Wildlife
    Refuge," typescript, Rachel Carson papers, Rachel Car-
    son Council, p. 3.
7. Quoted in Paul Brooks, *Speaking for Nature: How Literary
    Naturalists from Henry Thoreau to Rachel Carson Have Shaped
    America* (Boston: Houghton Mifflin, 1980), p. xiv.
8. *Time*, review of *Silent Spring*, 28 September 1962, pp. 45,
    48.
9. Carson, "Design."
10. Detailed history and evaluation of nature writing is avail-
    able in dissertations: Walter John Herrscher, "Some Ideas
    in Modern American Nature Writing" (Ph.D. disserta-
    tion, University of Wisconsin, 1969) incorporates infor-
    mation from Philip M. Hicks, "The Development of the
    Natural History Essay in America" (Ph.D. dissertation,
    University of Pennsylvania, 1924) and Judson McGehee,
    "The Nature Essay as a Literary Genre: An Intrinsic
    Study of the Works of Six English and American Nature
    Writers" (Ph.D. dissertation, University of Michigan,
    1958), but concentrates his own study on Carson, Der-
    leth, Krutch, Leopold, and White; Kenneth Johnson,
    "The Lost Eden: The New World in American Nature
    Writing" (Ph.D. dissertation, University of New Mexico,
    1973) focuses on the ideas of Krutch, Bartram, Thoreau,
    Muir, and Carson. Paul Brooks, *Speaking for Nature*, pro-
    vides some background material, as does Edwin Way

Teale in the introduction to his anthology, *Green Treasury, A Journey Through the World's Great Nature Writing* (New York: Dodd, Mead, 1952).

11. Teale, *Green Treasury*, p. xii.

12. Rachel Carson, "The Land Around Us," *This Week* (magazine section of the *New York Herald Tribune* and other newspapers), 25 May 1952.

13. H. M. Tomlinson, *Tide Marks* (New York and London: Harper & Brothers, 1924), p. 262.

14. John D. Margolis, *Joseph Wood Krutch: A Writer's Life* (Knoxville: University of Tennessee Press, 1980), pp. 154–55,

15. Rachel Carson, Autobiographical Sketch in *New York Herald Tribune Book Review*, 7 October 1951, p. 4.

16. Rachel Carson, "A Treasure Chest of Sea Books," *Washington Post*, 2 December 1951 (other newspapers on other dates); "Sea Leaves its Mark on World Poets," *Chicago Tribune*, 2 December 1951 (folder of articles by Carson, Rachel Carson collection, Beinecke Library, Yale University).

17. Henry Beston, *Especially Maine: The Natural World of Henry Beston from Cape Cod to the St. Lawrence*, selected and with introductions by Elizabeth Coatsworth (Brattleboro, Vt.: Stephen Greene Press, 1970), p. 24.

18. Coatsworth, in Beston, *Especially Maine*, pp. 2, 4.

19. Beston, *Especially Maine*, p. 25.

20. John Muir, *My First Summer in the Sierra* (Boston: Houghton Mifflin, 1911), pp. 28–29.

21. Stewart L. Udall, "The Legacy of Rachel Carson," *Saturday Review* 47 (16 May 1964): 23.

22. Rachel Carson, "Of Man and The Stream of Time" (commencement address, Scripps College, Claremont, Calif., 1962), Scripps College *Bulletin*, July 1962, p. 8 (offprint supplied through the courtesy of the college).

23. Stanley J. Kunitz, ed., *Twentieth Century Authors*, First Supplement, (New York: H. W. Wilson, 1955), p. 175.

24. Biographical material provided to Oxford University Press, 1950, in Brooks, *House of Life*, p. 4; review of Maurice Burton, *Margins of the Sea, New York Herald Tribune*, November 1954, in ibid.

25. Rachel Carson, "Underwater Explorers" (review of James Dugan, *Man Under the Sea*), *New York Times Book Review*, 13 May 1956, p. 5.

26. Rachel L. Carson, "The Dark Green Waters" (review of Gilbert C. Klingel, *The Bay*), *New York Times Book Review*, 14 October 1951, pp. 4, 20.

27. Rachel Carson, "From Trilobites to Dinosaurs to Men" (review of Jacquetta Hawkes, *A Land*), folder of articles by Carson, Rachel Carson collection, Beinecke Library, Yale University.

28. Robert van den Bosch, *The Pesticide Conspiracy* (Garden City, N.Y.: Doubleday, 1978).

29. Brooks, *House of Life*, p. 1.

30. *New York Times*, 16 April 1964.

31. Douglas M. Costle, "Women and the Environment," *EPA Journal* 4 (November–December 1978): 4.

32. William Beebe, *The Book of Naturalists, An Anthology of the Best Natural History* (New York: Alfred A. Knopf, 1944).

33. Beebe, *Book of Naturalists*, p. 87.

34. Henry Hill Collins, Jr., ed., *The American Year* (New York: G. P. Putnam's Sons, 1961), p. 42.

Bibliography

Primary Sources

Carson, Rachel L. *Under the Sea-Wind: A Naturalist's Picture of Ocean Life*. New York: Simon and Schuster, 1941.
———. *The Sea Around Us*. New York: Oxford University Press, 1951.
———. *Under the Sea-Wind: A Naturalist's Picture of Ocean Life*. New ed. with corrections. New York: Oxford University Press, 1952.
———. *The Edge of the Sea*. Boston: Houghton Mifflin, 1955.
———. *The Sea Around Us*. Rev. ed. New York: Oxford University Press, 1961.
New preface and notes.
———. *Silent Spring*. Boston: Houghton Mifflin, 1962.
———. *The Sense of Wonder*. New York and Evanston: Harper & Row, 1965.

Secondary Sources

Anticaglia, Elizabeth. "Rachel Carson." In *Twelve American Women*, pp. 208–24. Chicago: Nelson-Hall, 1975.
Brooks, Paul. *The House of Life: Rachel Carson at Work*. Boston: Houghton Mifflin, 1972.
Includes selections from her writings, both published and unpublished.
———. *Speaking for Nature: How Literary Naturalists from Henry Thoreau to Rachel Carson Have Shaped America*. Boston: Houghton Mifflin, 1980.
"Carson, Rachel Louise." In *Twentieth Century Authors*, First Supplement, edited by Stanley J. Kunitz, pp. 174–75. New York: H. W. Wilson, 1955.

151

Downs, Robert B. "Upsetting the Balance of Nature." In *Books that Changed America*, pp. 260–68. New York: Macmillan, 1970. *Silent Spring* is included among twenty-five books that have "played key roles in shaping the American world of today."

Gartner, Carol B. "Rachel Louise Carson." In *American Women Writers From Colonial Times to the Present: A Critical Reference Guide*, edited by Lina Mainiero, Vol. I., pp. 301–6. New York: Frederick Ungar, 1979.

"The Gentle Storm Center." *Life*, 12 October 1962, pp. 105–6, 109–10.
    Picture-story, Carson and *Silent Spring*.

Graham, Frank, Jr. "Rachel Carson." *EPA Journal* 4 (1978): 5–7, 38.

———. *Since Silent Spring*. Boston: Houghton Mifflin, 1970.
    A study of the use of pesticides; discussion of Rachel Carson's life and work.

Herrscher, Walter John. "Some Ideas in Modern American Nature Writing." Ph.D. dissertation, University of Wisconsin, 1969.
    Discusses Rachel Carson, August Derleth, Joseph Wood Krutch, Aldo Leopold, and E. B. White.

Johnson, Kenneth. "The Lost Eden: The New World in American Nature Writing." Ph.D. dissertation, University of New Mexico, 1973.
    Discusses William Bartram, Rachel Carson, Joseph Wood Krutch, John Muir, and Henry David Thoreau.

Pettis, Louis William. "Recent Approaches to Nature: Viewpoints of Selected American Non-Fiction Nature Writers, 1945–1964." Ph.D. dissertation, George Peabody College for Teachers, 1965.
    Discusses Marston Bates, William Beebe, Hal Borland, Rachel Carson, Alan Devoe, Joseph Wood Krutch, Aldo Leopold, Lorus Johnson Milne, Donald Culross Peattie, and Edwin Way Teale.

"Rachel Carson." In *World Who's Who in Science, From Antiquity to the Present*. Chicago: Marquis, 1968.

Seif, Dorothy Thompson. "The Legacy of Rachel Carson—Wonder, Awareness, and Warning: Pennsylvania College for Women 1928–29." Unpublished typescript. Rachel Carson papers, Rachel Carson Council, Washington, D.C.

Sterling, Philip. *Sea and Earth: The Life of Rachel Carson.* New York: Thomas Y. Crowell, 1970.

Juvenile; Women of America series.

Whorton, James. *Before Silent Spring: Pesticides and Public Health in Pre-DDT America.* Princeton, N.J.: Princeton University Press, 1974.

Discusses approach and impact of *Silent Spring.*

Wild, Peter. "Elder of the Tribe, Rachel Carson." *Backpacker* 30 (1978–1979): 26–28 + .

Index